CODES FOR ASCENSION:
Living New Earth Now

Expanding, Evolving and
Living as Light Beings

By Samantha SolBright Rodriguez

Copyright © 2022 Samantha SolBright Rodriguez

All rights reserved.

ISBN: 9780578373324

Cover design by: Samantha SolBright Rodríguez and Lucía Ramirez Martinez

To my family for all your pure love, support and encouragement, for challenging me, activating me, honoring me and accepting me for who I am and what I am becoming.

To my Soul siSTARS, for supporting my Soul journey, for the space we have held for one another no matter how near or far we live, for the pure love you have shown me as I continue to grow and remember all that we are.

To my Soul Brothers, human partners and twins for you have assisted me in opening up my heart in more ways than you may realize

To my Light/Soul family for allowing me to grow, expand, unite, share and play with you more and more as we evolve into who we are.

To everyone on their awakening and ascension path, thank you for allowing yourself to remember, to open and to live in a whole new way.

May these codes and activations continue to support us all in every way.

CONTENTS

INTRODUCTION	1
ALLOW	8
SURRENDER	10
TRUST	15
IMAGINE	20
LOVE	25
DISSOLVE	30
FEEL/SENSE	36
EMBRACE	42
ACCEPT	46
OPEN	54
PURIFY	61
UNIFY	65
MERGE	68
BE	72
DO	76
REALIGN	78
REMEMBER	81

BRIDGE	84
RELEASE	86
RE-CONNECT	90
RESOLVE	93
ANCHOR	96
RELAX	99
BALANCE	103
REPAIR	106
COMPLETE	109
COMMAND	115
BELIEVE	119
RESTORE	123
BREATHE	126
SHARE	130
PLAY	135
OBSERVE	139
INTENT	143
MOVE/WALK/JUMP	146
MOVE/SING/DANCE	151
MOVE/SPEAK/WRITE	155

CRY/SCREAM	160
CREATE	164
BUILD	173
FLIP	180
FLY/FLOAT	186
CLEAN	191
STAND UP	194
SLEEP	198
APPRECIATE	202
RESPECT	206
LISTEN	209
FOLLOW	213
LEAD	218
ENCOURAGE	221
SIMPLE	225
RETREAT	230
PATIENCE	234
SUPPORT	237
MELT	247
MEDITATE	251

SHINE	254
SHIFT	258
TOOLS FOR ASCENSION	261
WRITTEN ACTIVATIONS	277
I AM OPEN	278
YOU ARE TRULY SUPPORTED	280
CONTINUAL REBIRTH	283
THE BRIDGEKEEPER OF WORLDS	285
THE MASTER IN YOU	287
WE ARE ENERGY	289
GIVE YOURSELF PERMISSION	292
KEEP GOING!	293
SUPPORT OPPORTUNITIES	294
ABOUT THE AUTHOR	295
BOOKS BY THE AUTHOR	297

INTRODUCTION

The Ascension path is one of many twists, turns, reversals, realizations, revelations and discoveries that may not make a lot of sense to the human, linear, logical mind. There are many paradoxes, opposites, backwards and inside out paradigms that one will realize and come to remember all along the way that will assist our own ascension process. You don't have to comprehend it, you don't have to understand any of it while you're going through it, you don't need to try to fit it in any box, all you have to do is open your mind, heart and body to it and all will unfold in the most beautiful and magical way.

Ascension is a journey of many processes, it is a marathon not a sprint, it is a never ending evolution that will continue to bring forth higher and higher dimensional realms into our physical existence here. It is an inner frequency that we already hold within but that it is buried deep within the separated aspects and suppressed emotions that we hold deep inside our human vessel.

We are all here to make way for a New Golden Age, a New Earth Society, a New Earth Collective where our Light can reign again in every aspect and on every level. We are making way for our pure Power, Wisdom and Love to live fully in our bodies and no longer be suppressed.

Allow yourself to open up fully to this process, to this experience and to this evolutionary transition that we are all a part of. The more you allow your whole mind and body to surrender to this process and find joy in everything the faster things will shift inside and "out there."

This book of codes will further assist you in activating a deep Soul remembrance of what you already hold within. Allow yourself to absorb it without needing to fully comprehend it all with your mind for it's in the anchoring of the frequency of the codes that more will start to make sense. Remind yourself that you already hold the keys and codes in your body and DNA and all you have to do now is activate them so they can start to function as they were always intended to.

Keep opening up your mind, your heart, your field, your body and all that you are so that you can continue to remember who you are and all that you hold within.

Ascension

The frequency on this planet is being raised more and more every day and in every way, as this occurs the level of consciousness of every being on this planet is also being raised. The human species has operated under a much contracted state of consciousness which created a very limiting experience often referred as hell. Our linear/ego minds have taken control in a way that has created a lot of havoc, chaos, pain and suffering because of the perceived existence of fear and lack. Now after many linear years the veil is finally being lifted through the amount of Light that is pouring through the planet. What is creating this wave of Light? Many things, but one of the most important facets is where the planet is navigating in the Universe. It is traveling a new journey through what we refer to as the Photon belt. This is a belt that contains a large amount of photonic Light. As Gaia continues to travel deeper and deeper into this Photon Belt an increasing amount of Light frequencies will continue to pour down on this planet that will support a New Earth reality.

Perceive these Light frequencies as lamps, flashlights, lit candles that are bringing light to a very dark room. The more Light that enters this dark room the more one is able to see all that was hidden and suppressed; the more we regain our memory, the more we become more conscious and make different choices. The Light pouring on Gaia will create a new conscious human species that will operate from a completely different level of consciousness and will free every being living on her. This is part of the ascension process that is underway. Everything is ascending in consciousness so that we can rebuild the structural foundation of our society and create one that is built on purity, peace and love.

Light Encoded Information

These Light frequencies come with what we refer as light codes. Light codes are packets of energy that carry Divine information used to reconfigure the entire human body/template/field/system. This Divine information is like a new instruction manual and with it our body is receiving an upgrade from the old instruction manual/3D matrix system. This old instruction manual was basically corrupted and it created a reality that was based on distortion and separation. Our 12 strand DNA has been dormant and shut down and this is mainly why our bodies haven't been able to sustain as much of our Soul/Light inside of the body; the physical body was just too dense, too polluted, too contracted with emotions, beliefs and structures that take up much room in our bodies. As these light codes are allowed to come into the body, the DNA begins to rewrite itself and as this occurs the density of the body begins to release and the body is able to hold more Light.

The more Light that enters the body, the more our bodies begin to wake up, activate and clear the emotional/mental/physical density that has been stored inside of our body which created many imbalances, sickness, dis-eases and much more. These light codes literally have the ability to repair every cell, every organ, every molecule and every DNA strand down to its core. This is the power that Light holds and it is the power that we have as Light Beings. We are much more than this body, we are Light, we are purity, we are love and now that we are waking up to this it is time to work in harmony with our bodies so that we can fully return to living as a Soul and expand beyond the limitations of the old 3D reality.

New Earth

New Earth is what is being birth from every single one of us; it is the frequency of pure Light that we hold that creates this version of Gaia. The old 3D matrix is disintegrating before our very eyes and it is all happening because we are allowing more Light to come through into our bodies. Yes, our bodies hold/held the physical structures that created and sustained the 3D realms and as we continue to dissolve all of the separation, clear our fears and lack based mentalities from our vessel we have the opportunity to create Heaven on earth.

Each person gets to create this in their own personal reality before we get to see it in a global scale. We each have to hold, anchor, sustain and stabilize the Light frequencies inside of our body and then re-align, re-prioritize, re-access, remove and re-create everything in our physical world so that every aspect supports our Light, amplifies peace and brings Unity in every way.

New Earth is a reality that already exists, it is a frequency, a state of consciousness that we each must choose to operate from; it doesn't matter where you live, where you go, what you do, who you're with because New Earth is inside, it is what you bring forward as Light. You have the opportunity now to experience a New Earth reality exactly where you are the more you open your heart and mind, the more you expand your perspective, the more you allow yourself to honor your emotions and thoughts and dissolve every aspect that still lives in separation. Yes, it's a journey, a marathon not an overnight process but the more you open in every way and in every moment you can start to experience the beauty and magic right before your very eyes.

This is what we are all creating through our conscious choices and through the continual release and dissolution of the old. You may still see the old world being portrayed in the media and news but the more you hold your Light, embrace the ascension path fully and no longer feed or judge the fear based agendas your reality will be completely different. The less we hold on to the old, the less we focus on it, the less we feed it and support it the less and less real it will become. We innerstand that what is happening in the old world is still serving a purpose for many and we respect everyone's journey but as we all become more conscious the more we remember that we don't have to participate in the old world in order to create a new one.

This is where we must all allow it to fall, to break, to collapse in the way that it needs to and continue to focus on the New, the New ways, the New systems, the New foundations that we each get to create in our own individual realities first. When we create a New Earth in our own physical realities we are building the foundational stability inside of our body and as we do that we are able to then expand it in a much bigger and greater scale. Again, it is a process that takes many linear years to fully achieve in our own reality but this is how it all starts and as this continues we will have the necessary codes, templates and sacred knowledge held in our bodies to fully live in Unity Consciousness as a collective.

Invitation

I invite you to follow your own flow, let go of the need to read it in the order that I wrote it for each code is just as equally important and it will activate much within in the moment you need it. Every code holds specific codes and frequencies that are meant to assist you in unlocking more at a deeper level. Allow yourself to be guided each time you pick up the book and let your body, Soul/Light guide you and trust that the pages you read are perfect for you. Allow yourself to dive deeper into each code on your own, feeling more, seeing more, observing how each code plays out in your reality, asking yourself/your body more questions so you can open up even more. If you feel called to utilize each word like a daily decree, or in meditation and just sit with it, feel the resistance or any heaviness attached to each word/code so that you can uncover more of the frequencies that may be blocking you from fully opening up to it. Grab yourself a drawing pad and colored pencils and start writing notes, messages, guidance that comes through as you read each one and start playing with your own reality so you can start to observe/feel the codes that are coming through for you to activate, play and anchor.

Everything is essentially a code, a key, a frequency, an activation that is supporting you and assisting you in so many ways. Open yourself more and more in every way so that you can start to decipher and read your own codes in your own field/reality. Continue to open up all of your senses so that you can start to feel everything with your whole entire

body, this will assist in expanding you more and reconnecting with everything so that you can recognize the purpose in all.
Last but certainly not least, injoy, have fun and keep embracing it all!

CODES FOR ASCENSION

ALLOW

    Every time you breathe you allow the air to flow through you, in and out, you don't have to think about it, analyze it, understand it, it's just something we allow ourselves to do. We allow ourselves to go with this flow, to go with the rhythm of our bodies, our lungs and our heart and it's this beautiful effortless symphony and harmony. When our minds don't get in the way it is quite simple to just let go and allow. This energy is one of the most important ones to fully invite, welcome, embrace and embody because the more that you do the smoother the ride becomes. There are many things about this journey that won't make sense to the linear human mind and they're not supposed to; this is because this gives us an opportunity to let go of trying to figure it all out or understand it from the perspective of the mind and just open up and fully trust. Our human minds will only be able to grasp a fraction of what is actually occurring and if you stop and try to think about everything you won't get very far.

    This entire process is about letting yourself open up to the experience with your body and all of your senses instead of just with your mind. In fact if you stay stuck in your mind, you're going to run yourself in circles, you won't understand all that is going on and you'll become very exhausted. When you let yourself drop down into your heart space and your body you start to open up more, allow more and trust more because as you do you will start to remember that your body is supporting you in this entire process. Your LightBody is assisting you in your ascension journey, it is clearing, re-coding, re-calibrating things that your linear mind can't possible do at this time with the knowledge that it has because it is just very limited.

One of the easiest things you can start to do that will assist you in opening up more to allowing is to tune in to your breath. When you tune in to your breath you get to connect with the parts/aspects of your body that are already in flow with this frequency, they are already dancing with the organic rhythm of the lungs without your mind getting in the way. As you give yourself permission to move, flow, dance, sway, fly, navigate with this energy you'll start to feel and embody it with your whole body/mind/field and whatever frequency/reality/experience you are attempting to allow in your field will start to flow as well. Allowing the flow of ALL energies/frequencies is going to be super important throughout your entire journey because we have been so constricted/limited/small in so many ways and in many aspects.

We've blocked, controlled, hindered, stopped, judged and contracted the flow of all energies inside of our bodies and as a result this created a lot of chaos in our internal world as well as our "external" world. When we hold tight to this energy we stop the natural flow in which energy moves and we grab on to the idea that we need to control the energy in order to obtain/gain a specific result when in reality this creates more friction/restriction /resistance and so many other things that actually make it harder to shift/re-align the energy. In other words it creates the opposite effect of what we are attempting to achieve.

Instead the more we open up, allow and create more space, more room, more expansion in every part of our body/field/reality the easier the flow, movement, release and re-alignment of all channels of energy. As a result the frequencies that need to be cleared and released from the body are now able to move out and the frequencies that we need to invite/welcome in to shift our reality will easily start to appear/activate to assist us in whatever we are ready to create.

Continue to connect to the frequency of allowing, remind your body/mind to continuously allow and open up to this flow and the more you do the more you'll be able to shift and create things much quicker than before.

SURRENDER

The ascension journey is about a constant, continual and conscious surrender; surrendering to your Light, your Soul, Your LightBody and your path. We have a misperception that surrendering may seem/feel like it's a bad thing, it holds a negative connotation if you look at it from the context of losing or giving up something or someone that is perceived to be more powerful than you. Yet as we evolve out of the old constructs and systems we start to see things a little bit different. This isn't a surrendering as in a loss but rather surrendering to the aspect of yourself that knows more, remembers more, is much more conscious and aware than you are in that moment.

All of us have allowed our emotions, our old beliefs, our old limitations, our ego aspects to take control of much of our lives and that has created very unbalanced, unhappy, ego –aligned realities that don't serve or support our Soul/Higher Self aspect instead feed our fear, lack and judgment.

We are now moving out of this way of doing/being to a much more Soul-aligned existence and in order to accomplish this we have to fully surrender to our Higher Heart/Soul/Light/Higher Self and every Higher aspect of ourselves. Our mind/ego has run the show for far too long and in the bigger spectrum of things it has created a system where pain, chaos, suffering, competition, lack, fear, suppression, oppression have dominated the majority of our world leaving us feeling unfulfilled, unhappy, unworthy and so many other things.

Things are changing now. We are becoming so much more aware of who we are, who we've always been, what we are capable and we are just scratching the surface of it all. Our Source Creator potential hasn't even been fully tapped in nor discovered and so there is much uncharted territory as we continue to evolve and remember. It becomes crucial for all of us to continually let go of what the mind still perceives as true, for it still functions from a dualistic mentality that is very limited from how things actually are. We have surrendered to our minds/ego/human brain for far too long because we created the 3D reality that functioned primarily from the left brain, the linear, the logic, the rational which separated it completely from the right brain, the intuitive, the emotional, the imaginative, the creative.

This separation of brains/mentalities/concepts has also created much separation in our physical reality where we have placed much more importance, power, credibility to things/concepts/ideas/beliefs that can be explained by the left brain only. Do you see/feel how limiting this is? A reality where you only believe something to be true based on whether it can be explained from the logical side of the brain leaves so much on the table that can only be explained by the right side of the brain. So needless to say yes, we have discarded, disregarded, gaslighted, disbelieved so many experiences that go way beyond what our linear/left/ego mind can perceive and comprehend at this time. Just because something doesn't make sense or can't be physically proven at this moment in our history by the left brain doesn't make it false, untrue, evil, wicked, or dark and the exciting part is that more and more people are starting to open up, embrace and remember that there is more to life than what can be seen with just our physical eyes or explained by our linear/logical brain.

Surrendering to new possibilities, new ideas, new truths, new points of view, new meanings, new worlds, new perspectives, new realities and new concepts is only the beginning. Like I mentioned there is still so much that is still yet to be discovered, explored, remembered and embraced and we are on the path to it all. Things won't stop now in fact they will only continue to accelerate more and more and more as the old realities continue to change, collapse, de-construct and no longer be tolerated by Humanity. In fact old earth was constructed on linear/ego/left brain ideals, concepts, beliefs and systems so the more we start to open up to ALL new systems and perspectives the more the old falls away with nothing to hold on to. Yes, it all has to do with how each and every single one of us start to change our own perceptions and perspectives, because what we hold inside is what creates the "external" world. As we start to embrace and surrender to the world of energy, intuition, creativity, Love, peace, unity, joy and magic (all right brain core values) we start to see/create a world that upholds those same frequencies and systems.

Again the ego mind/brain functions from a very limited perspective where it believed it had to surrender to an "outside" power, authority figure, control system and old structures and as we move out of this part of our brain and move into our intuitive/sensitive/creative/Soul connected/right brain we start to see things very, very different. We start to remember that things have been very backwards indeed, we start to remember that the true power is actually held within each and every single one of us and as we take our power back we have the ability to change our reality and the entire world. This is where we start to no longer believe in the ego/victim/powerless/small/contracted part of ourselves but rather the Higher Self/Light/Soul aspect that fully recognizes its true power, potential, truth and higher purpose.

As we continue to surrender to this aspect of ourselves we no longer allow the old to control, demean, disempower, manipulate, and contract us in any way, shape or form. One of the reasons we surrendered to the old is because for the most part we didn't know that there was any other way to survive, we weren't fully conscious nor remembered that we had a choice, we thought that we had to go with the flow of how things have always been in the "past", but as we/humanity awakens more and more and start to see beyond the veil, wake up, become more conscious we start to make different choices, we start to only allow the frequencies that fully support us and amplify our pure Light. This is part of the great shift of/in HUmanity that is currently taking place on the planet right now and it is beyond exciting to see.

The Left and Right Brain

As our bodies continue to evolve, the right brain and left brain will become more balanced, merged and unified. Yes, many biological and physiological aspect of our body are changing, shifting and evolving beyond what we innerstand or even believe. This merging and unification will allow us to function from both side of the brain in unison and harmony; we are creating a new quantum, Divine logic and reasoning where seeing things from an energetic, vibrational and frequency aspect will become the norm instead of just a concept or a theory.

We are all waking up to a completely new way of seeing and perceiving and it will change everything. The more we open up and remember that everything is energy, the more we will start to value it. There is so much yet to be seen and remembered and it is very fascinating indeed.

The LightBody

As we start to ascend, there is a phase where we start to activate our LightBodies. This is the Light of your body coming online inside instead of just floating "out there", it is also the merger of all four bodies (mental, emotional, spiritual and physical), the full embodiment of your Light, the clearing of all density and the dissolution of your old human carbon-based body. The LightBody is the energy body that is able to fully allow the Soul to live inside the human vessel as well as fully expand "outside" of the body; it is us becoming full crystals again and operating from a much higher level of consciousness than before. This is just a very simple, short explanation as it entails a lot more as it continues to evolve. What's important to mention here is that the surrendering to your Light/LightBody is also an extremely important part of the process. We mentioned above the surrendering of your right brain and Soul/Light/Higher Self and this also includes the LightBody because they actually become one and the same. The LightBody however goes through many physical sensations, changes, upgrades, clearings that go beyond what the human/linear mind can comprehend and also beyond what the medical community/professionals can also explain at this moment.

The LightBody is currently coming online for every single person on this planet whether they realize it, believe it, are conscious of it or not, it does not matter because the amount of Light coming through into the planet is astronomically higher than what's it's ever been in a very long time. There are many people feeling weird, bizarre sensations in their body that not even doctors can explain and that is why it is important to remember that many sensations that are happening to the body don't fit in the old perceptions and boxes. This is why surrendering to the LightBody will assist you in not just having a smoother experience but you will also be assisting the LightBody in all that it is trying to do aka clear, release, dissolve, re-code, re-balance, etc. Our minds have really no clue as to what is going on and they are not supposed to assist because they still function from fear and lack. Continue to completely surrender to your LightBody/Higher Self and as you do you will be releasing the need to control/manipulate the process and hence releasing all resistance towards it.

TRUST

In a world where everything is geared towards respecting and accepting the "outside" world and their advice, knowing, information rather than ones' own guidance, inner truths, wisdom and knowledge learning to trust yourself is one of the most important aspects of this entire journey. We have been disconnected from our own compass, our own Soul, our own body in every aspect and therefore we have learned to not listen to ourselves. This has been detrimental to our own being, our physical/mental/emotional health in more ways than we can comprehend with our minds but as we start to reconnect with the purity of our hearts we will start to see and innerstand how much this has affected us in many ways.

We must return to trusting in our own selves, our body, our Soul/Higher Self and our inner knowing rather than always giving it away to things/people outside of ourselves. The "outside" narrative will never have the knowledge or the experiences that you have, it will never know you as well as your body/heart/Soul knows you because these aspects are you.

Coming into this human existence we learn from a very early age to rely solely on others mainly because at the beginning we are not able to support ourselves. Our human parents/guardians/family members become our sole providers and supporters along the way, this creates a belief/program that others know more therefore we need to trust more on things/people/authorities outside of ourselves. As we grow up we slowly start to do things for ourselves, at the beginning it's just the basic needs, and as we continue on this human experience we start to learn more ways in which to support ourselves more and more. Some of these things go against the norm or against what our parents believe or want for us and we either fall back in pleasing our human parents or we follow our own journey. In any way, we don't often gain full trust in ourselves for many other reasons.

This journey is about rediscovering ourselves, empowering ourselves and having a deep sacred connection with every part of ourselves because all answers are deeply held inside of the body. Of course this isn't quite what we're taught just yet. We come to believe that others know more about ourselves, our own body, our own needs and wants better than we do. How could this possible be true if we are far beyond a cookie cutter model, each of us is a unique individual with unique traits, history, background, lineage and purposes. Each body has a distinct amount of Light that it chose to carry before incarnating and therefore each LightBody goes through different things based on the Light quotient and Soul purposes that each chooses.

As we each continue to connect with every part of our body, every aspect and every reality we hold inside we each become more in tuned with what our body needs. Our LightBodies are Divine Intelligence, just think about how our subconscious minds are able to operate and control every function of our most vital organs without us having any awareness of it. We fully allow, surrender and trust in our subconscious to do what it does best while we continue to focus on other things in our lives. Our bodies know exactly what to do, what they need, what amount is appropriate in that moment and so much more. The caveat is that since our DNA has been tampered it doesn't quite function the way that it needs to because the program it runs on is a distorted one of fear, lack and separation.

As we continue and allow these Light codes to come through and activate/repair our entire DNA system fully our entire bodies will go through the necessary upgrades, recoding, recalibration that is needed to fully restore purity and balance at a deep cellular level. The beauty is that your DNA functions like your subconscious in that it knows exactly what to do if we just allow and surrender fully to the process. We don't need to know exactly what is going on, why it's happening, why we are feeling a certain way, what are the ins and out, we don't need to make it fit into an old 3D box to make sense of it in fact quite the opposite. The more we ask from a linear mindset/ fear, the more we inter-fear with the process, the more we create resistance and the harder it is for the body to fully do its job.

As we come to regain trust in ourselves, we must restore trust within our own bodies and our own Soul/Light as well. Throughout the ascension process the body will continuously go through a re-tuning, clearing, anchoring, integration process that is vast, immense and complex. Our linear minds cannot even begin to comprehend all that it entails because of where it functions from and so we must challenge ourselves to not let the human mind control the process and be devoured by the fear of not knowing what is going on. This is where the ego mind must come to be comfortable with the unknown, the weird, the bizarre, the crazy and the trippy experiences that all come with the ascension process. This is where as humans we must return to fully trusting in our LightBody and the process that our bodies go through to become pure Light anchored in the body.

At the moment this goes far beyond the notions and knowings of the normal medical community as they yet don't quite accept/comprehend the energetics of the body. We have to be able to move past the old constructs of the old reality and everything that was built on them including western medicine. Remember that the basis of western medicine are extremely young and it will take a massive reconstruction of their foundations to bring it up to speed to the new ways of 5D and above. This will occur as everything re-aligns with New Earth and old earth continues to collapse more, but as of right now the more we detach from the old systems the more we support our body in its evolution.

Our purpose is to continue to connect with our bodies so that we can be in full Divine Union with all that we are and as we do we will start to be fully allowing and receptive of the messages that come through from the body. As we continue to dissolve separation inside and all the emotional heaviness we start to regain trust back in ourselves, we start to honor and respect others opinions and knowledge but we no longer dismiss our own inner knowing and our bodies needs and wants because we are no longer compromising our Soul in any way. Yes, we used to compromise our Souls needs and wants in many ways in the 3D/4D realities and many times because we didn't know any better; we were still blindfolded to all the Divine Knowledge that our bodies hold within and so instead of talking or asking our bodies what they needed we consulted with others and took their knowing as the only truth. Not to say that it's not true but it's only true from one dimension, one angle and one perspective and there are a multitude of other truths and perspectives because we are multidimensional and we don't operate just from one dimension. Our bodies are able to tap into different dimensions and truths the more Light we hold and the more expanded we are but if we only ask one source outside of ourselves that only operates from a closed/contracted/linear state of consciousness then the truth will be very different from let's say someone with a higher level of consciousness.

At the beginning when we are first learning how to tune into our body we often connect with those on a similar frequency to receive our answers but even then it's always best to go back inside and tune in to the purity of your heart and check. Your body will always support you and it is important to remember this and remind ourselves constantly of this as well.

Listening with our Whole Body

The linear mind will give you messages that are different than the messages you receive from your Higher Heart (located in your thymus gland). One of the best ways to start to connect and listen to the body is to fully tune out the linear mind, closing our eyes and placing our hand on our higher heart area to receive the messages that are fully in tuned with our Higher guidance.

For most of our journey we've been listening to the mind, the logical part of ourselves that always tried to conform to the old ways and old systems. There are many aspects of us still inside and so we may still receive messages from aspects that are still separated, wounded and unhealed. Don't suppress anything. This is where honoring these aspects and allowing them to fully come out and express themselves in every way that is appropriate and safe is going to greatly assist you in this process. Think of these aspects as just needing to get that energy out, they need a safe outlet in which to express themselves and feel loved and supported; after they are able to get it all out of their system the body starts to rebalance itself and reintegrate these separated aspects back inside. As this occurs your Higher Self aspects are able to come through to relay the messages and guidance that are pure. In many cases these lower self aspects block us from being able to hear or receive the Higher Self Guidance that is held deep within the body and so as you continue to hold sacred space for them you will release all the suppressed energy still held inside and interference seizes to exist. Your Higher Heart opens up more, your body relaxes and your body is able to relay the necessary messages that you need in order to trust more in the process.

Remember that a lot of the times the messages will be simple, yet very assuring and loving. At first you won't have access to in-depth information of what is all going on in the body. You build up to this and it all starts by creating/building and establishing a solid foundation of pure trust within you and your LightBody. The more you open up and just trust that your LightBody isn't here to harm you or hurt you but quite the opposite, it is here to fully support you and assist you in this massive process the more you start to open up to receive more bits of information.

Again the more you trust in the process and in your LightBody the more it trusts you and the more it starts to unlock more information deeply held within for you to share and assist others. We are finally moving away from abusing and suppressing our bodies like we once did and fully honoring, respecting, listening and embracing every part of who we are in every way.

IMAGINE

Imagination is one of the greatest gifts that we have, it is so powerful in creating everything and yet it becomes one of the most forgotten concepts that we begin to lose as we grow up. The artist Pablo Picasso said it so perfectly, "Everything you imagine is real", which brings us into divine a bit deeper into the nature of reality.

Reality has been misperceived as something that you can only see, feel, hear, touch, smell with one or more of our human senses but yet our human senses only have a fraction of their true potential activated and so they aren't able to perceive everything in its entirety. Our linear brain is currently very limited and small; it can only perceive things from a contracted view instead of an expanded view like our higher heart.

When we open up our higher heart, we are instantly connected to the wonders of our higher mind and as they merge they activate a very powerful field force that knows no limits. The power of our imagination has no boundaries, it has no limitations and no set rules like our linear mind does. It goes beyond time and space and the more we utilize it the more we remember its power in our own reality.

The moment we imagine something it becomes real because it is instantly created and exists in the field, we may not automatically see it with our own physical eyes or touch it with our own physical hands but that does not matter for it is already in the realm of perception and that is enough for it to be real. Reality is far beyond what we have been taught in books or by the old concepts of science and we are finally remembering it all. Our imagination can create instantaneously and that is one of our many powers as Source Creator Beings. We are creators by nature and nothing can take that away, so now it is through our own inner sacred connection that we must take back our place as such and remember how to utilize our imagination in the most powerful of ways.

Dimensional Realms

There are far too many dimensional realms in this world to even count them all but needless to say there are many. Most dimensions cannot be perceived by our senses but one of the ways that we can is through our own inner imagination. Our imagination is connected to our right brain, this part of the brain is the creative, the intuitive, the artistic and hence it is directly in communication with the energy world, the world of Spirit, the etheric world that has been by far too long condemned to be nonexistent. Yet it exists and it always has. Our right brain has had a deep connection with it and the more that we activate our creative side the stronger and stronger it becomes to the degree that we are able to perceive it much more intensely.

Our imagination can open up to realms far yet to be believed and yet to be seen by our own physical eyes. It is through our imagination that our inner knowing, our intuition and our unique capabilities and gifts start to open up and be remembered. Yes, each and every single one of us has gifts far beyond this time but they have been suppressed for far too long because we have been too disconnected from our emotions, our bodies and our imagination.

Our ability to shift to different dimensions, different worlds, different realities is all locked up inside but can be unlocked by the usage of our imagination. Our imagination can be so pure and uninhibited, it has a power far greater than we can conceive but yet the more we utilize it the more we start to remember. Most of us grew up with the belief that imagination is just a child's play or a toy that once we turn a certain age it is meant to be long gone and forgotten. Our imagination is a very powerful key, a tool that is meant to be used in its purity no matter what our human age is perceived to be. Imagination is who we are, it is how we create a better world, it is how we can Light up this world and it is how we can bring back the magic that has been long forgotten by many.

There is a beautiful movie called "The Little Prince", that I watched not too long ago and there is a beautiful scene where the wiser gentleman says to the kid, "growing up is not the problem, forgotten is." It was such a powerful and activating phrase that is so very true for every single one of us. Growing up is not the problem, but forgetting who we are, forgetting how to play, forgetting how to use our imagination is one of the greatest misconception of our time that must be brought back.

Our inner child is locked up in our imagination, and when we stop imagining we also forget to communicate with this part of ourselves; it gets lost and forgotten and so in some aspect we do too. We become too busy to play, too busy to laugh, too stiff to dance, too rigid to draw, too judgmental to sing, we become to caught up in a reality that sucks our Light away without even becoming aware of it. We become so limited in our minds about what adults do and what kids do and we lose ourselves in the never ending loop cycle of adulthood. There isn't anything more detrimental to our well being than forgetting this very important aspect of ourselves that is always with us. You see just because we start to 'grow up' doesn't mean that our inner child disappears, in fact it is always here inside of us, wanting to play, wanting to sing, wanting to cry and yell and shout everything that it didn't get the opportunity to do when it was younger. This aspect of us doesn't go away and it never will. Our child aspects are yearning to come out and play, and talk and sing and communicate to our "older aspect" of ourselves that is lost and lonely in the world of adulthood.

Reconnecting with our inner child is part of everyone's journey and sometimes you won't know how that journey will be for you. For me, it has brought me back to my childhood home, my childhood room, my childhood neighborhood and I didn't even know that I needed to be back in this place to find my inner child again. There has been something so deeply special about coming back to this place, remembering things that I had long forgotten and feeling emotions that I didn't even know I still held deeply inside. This experience has been far more powerful than I could have possibly imagined but now I realize why I was led back to this place at this time; it all led me back to myself. I always wanted to come back home, I always dreamed and imagined coming back and now I know why I needed to come back.

Everyone has a different journey back to their inner child and it is perfect for every single one of us we just have to be open enough to venture and go all in and once we do it will be one that we never forget and never regret.

Divine Child

The Divine Child is deep inside our inner child, and this one is actually the one that must be activated but in order to get to get to it we must go through our inner child first. The inner child is the one that still has much to feel, much to say, much to express, much to release as it never got the chance and opportunity when it was growing up. This is the experience that we each chose prior to incarnation, and there is a higher purpose for that as well. As you begin to open up more and more you start to remember the ins and outs of our choices that even though as young children we completely forget about as a Soul we remember that we chose this for ourselves.

As we open up to our inner child, we will be opening up to many,

many emotions and feelings, many thoughts and beliefs and every single one of them must be felt in a way that creates more freedom inside. Every emotion that is released, every thought that is honored, every belief that is owned creates an opening, this opening becomes the door in which our inner child can merge back and it is how our Divine Child emerges from the shadows. It's always been there, just like our Light, but it was just buried and suppressed under all the darkness/emotions that we've been carrying.

Now more than ever we are finally starting to become the Divine Children that we've always been, the ones that know the importance of play, fun, joy, singing and imagining things in the purest of ways. The more we allow our Divine Child to come through the more we will change not only our lives but the entire planet, for it is in allowing our Divine Child and every Higher Self aspect to resurface that all is restored and brought back to the peace and joy that we truly are and that we truly hold inside.

LOVE

Love is an energy, it is the pure essence of who we are at our core. It isn't something weak or feeble but rather the frequency that makes up the entire reality of our existence. You see in our old 3D world love has been misconstrued, misinformed and misperceived to be something less than what it actually is. It isn't a lovey-dovey, ooey-gooey kind of thing only found in romance movies and fairy tales; it is far beyond our linear minds can truly come to innerstand.

Love is the most powerful force in the entire universe; it is creation itself and therefore the only thing that actually exists in its most purest form. Everything is created from this frequency and everything can be returned back to it as well. It is a powerful force hidden deep beneath us all and far greater than what we have been led to believe.

Because we are this pure essence there is an embodiment of this energy that we are all in the process of returning to. There is so much that comes forth that needs to be shifted and morphed back to this energy. The essence of becoming pure Love entails that we hold this frequency in every way and in every circumstance no matter what without reverting back to the old ways that we believed loved to be.

Loving something is far from allowing anything into one's reality. Becoming Love is being able to transform anything back to a state of openness and freedom. It may require firmness of character, boldness, strong aptitude, honesty, clarity, kindness brevity and anything else that is highest aligned in that moment. Love isn't about being nice and allowing the old to step and trample with our energy, our bodies and our Light, that was the old thought and belief system. In the old reality we were led to believe that love was soft, weak, fragile and that we had to protect ourselves. We thought that loving was allowing anyone and anything into our lives even if it was detrimental to our health, well-being and went against our Soul. This is actually opposite from what our pure essence is here to be and do and we are finally remembering.

Loving Ourselves

Love is a frequency we hold but yet we have forgotten to give that love to our very own being. We were taught to always give, give to others, help others and sometimes even give away our own energy, time, focus without giving any to ourselves or without replenishing ourselves with more. We have forgotten about ourselves, we have forgotten who we are and what are needs are as Light beings, thinking we aren't worthy enough to receive and that it is more important to give ourselves away to others instead of giving the very same thing to ourselves. Yes, it is a very backwards existence indeed and that is just how we allowed it to be for many reasons. But now we are starting to see the twistedness of it all, we are starting to decipher just how detrimental this has been in many ways and how misaligned and out of tune we were with our very own essence.

The love we have for ourselves has been small and conditional. We have been taught from a very young age that we must be a certain way, do certain things, say or not say certain words, dress a certain way in order to be acceptable, likeable, loveable and worthy of being supported. We learn from a very young age that we are not perfect just as we are, that being good enough and worthy has lots of terms and conditions, that we can't be ourselves, that we can't be happy just as we are and the list goes on and on and on. For this and many other things we learn to dislike ourselves, we learn not to love ourselves in the most purest way because we can never reach perfection in the eyes of society or the eyes of our parents, we can never be who the world wants us to be and therefore we shouldn't love ourselves as we are.

This is one of the most challenging things to overcome but by far one of the most important and integral parts of this entire journey and living experience. This is about going against the grain with everything that we have ever been taught about ourselves, this is about going beyond the rules and expectations that we slowly grow to adapt, accept, conform and respect in this world. This is truly about re-discovering who we truly are inside and becoming to love and respect every aspect of our being in every way no matter what others may say, think or believe. Every person has a role and every person was chosen by us to play a certain character for a specific reason that many of us are unaware of at the time but as we open up more and more to ourselves, more and more to who we are and what we are as pure Love we start to see things from a whole new way and a whole new perspective.

Open yourself to yourself, open yourself to this journey, open yourself to the purity of who you are and open yourself to every aspect and role and character you have ever played. Just open up to it, you don't have to agree with everything, you don't have to like everything, you don't have to believe everything, you don't have to do anything but just open up to it because when you do there is a magical and powerful thing that starts to occur. Being open to everything spirals out and allows every emotion, every belief, every heaviness, every distortion to become unstuck and unanchored from your body. This becomes a ripple effect that morphs and twists, untwists and recodes itself into a new way of perceiving things. You start to not only be open to yourself, but respect yourself, honor yourself, have care and compassion for everything you've ever been, said and done, you get to see yourself from a whole new set of eyes, you get to have an expanded vision of why you chose things, why you created things and you get to have a deeper inner-standing of yourself. Having deep sacred love for yourself becomes a natural and organic thing to do because you no longer see yourself as weak, small, evil, dark and ugly, those were just versions of yourself that you chose to play and now you get to return yourself back to the true version of who you are. You get to evolve out of those old characters and open your heart fully to becoming who you've always been.

As we becoming more loving and respectful of who we are and all that we've been then and only then do we get to have the same level of love and respect for everything and everyone that surrounds us. When we get to have that deep sacred connection and love towards every part of our being it becomes a natural and organic part of our existence and everything around us also get to feel and receive that same energy. The more connected we are with every part of ourselves, the more connected we will feel with everything and everyone and we start to have a deep sacred honor for all as well as they are merely a reflection of who we are.

Loving and respecting ourselves means loving and respecting every form of energy that is part of our reality and in that new awareness we get to inner-stand the inter-connectedness and how everything intertwines and creates our entire reality in every way, shape and form. Yes, our entire reality is constructed with the thread of love as a Creative force, and yet the less love and respect we have for everything and everyone around us the reality that gets reflected back to us is less than loving and respectful. When we open ourselves completely to ourselves and everything else we get to experience a pure and profound love for everything as is, for exactly what is showing us and for exactly the role we chose them to have. This openness is a form of deep love and respect and in that everything morphs and shifts and evolves into something much more beautiful and sacred that we get to love and respect just the same. The difference is that the reality that gets created from the love and respect we have is a completely different one than if we were not holding that love. Our reality gets to be one of pure love, joy, bliss and magic because that is how we choose to hold everything as and in that purity we get to create more magic and peace in our entire reality that allows for a more peaceful, sacred, respectful and harmonious experience for us and for the entire world for that creates a powerful ripple effect in the entire human gridding system that is felt, touched and perceived by all.

Yes, love is THAT powerful and way more powerful even still that we have barely scratched the surface of it all. The more we open up more and more in every way and in every level the more we get to remember just how it truly changes and Unifies all.

DISSOLVE

There will be many words that interlock and intertwine with one another but each will carry its own tone and frequency and new insights will come through for each. Dissolve is one of those words that co-relates with clear and cleanse and transfigure among many other words. These are words that relate to processes that are utilized all along the way to create more space inside. The dissolution of something takes many forms and facets and comes in many phases. At one level it is quick and simple but at a cellular/DNA level it is only the beginning of a much more intricate and vast process that takes much linear time for the entire body to complete. This is one of the many reasons why this is a journey, a vast, winding road that must be taken very consciously and that one must learn to enjoy in every way as that will create much more beauty and fulfillment in every phase. In one aspect it is a never ending journey for we keep growing and evolving and expanding in so many ways that we may not fully comprehend at this time. Many of us are here for the long run, we are here to make a huge and lasting impact on the entire planet and that is worth every phase.

So back to dissolve... this frequency has much power, it holds many keys and codes that the LightBody knows and understands in ways that the linear mind cannot. This frequency allows an opening in which the energy and force field become malleable, bendable and more breathe-able than before. There is a loosening of the gridding system that allows an interchangeable give and take with the energy that one is working with.

The heaviness that one is holding on to at any level becomes less heavy, it is as if the anchors holding it in place start to shift and unanchor this energy from the body in ways that support the expansion of your field.

Remember that everything that was/is still heavy inside of the body creates an impediment for the frequency of Light to flow and move in ways that are pure and natural. This isn't to say that Light isn't moving inside of you but it takes more effort, it is much slower and it is much more constricting when it is surrounded by a gridding system that doesn't fully support it. It is almost as if it were held with its hands tied behind its back unable to fully move and create in ways that are easy and simple.

As Light being in a body, we come here with a responsibility to assist the human vessel in ways that fully support it and fully expand its experience. Every single one of us have an enormous amount of heaviness inside and outside of the human physical body that must be released and dissolved so that our Light can live freely inside and so our LightBodies can fully assist us with the process of ascension. Everything from emotions, belief systems, constructs, thoughts, thought forms, grids and so much more have been built on a 3D level of consciousness that is very heavy to move around. As more Light pours into our planet the more we become aware of this heaviness. Many of us didn't see or feel it before, we were so caught up in living a life that we thought we needed to live, a reality that we thought would bring us much happiness and fulfillment, working hard to create titles, labels, identities, accolades, money and material accumulation of things that we thought we needed in our life. All of this becomes quite the opposite of what we once thought it was, the value of everything starts to change and shift in more ways that we expect at first and then we start to truly realize that nothing in our reality was truly in alignment with our Soul, our heart and our body. That is when our reality and our whole lives start to change and we become more and more aware of how out of alignment we were and how chaotic our lives truly are.

    The physical materialization of our reality is all tied up to our own belief systems and especially the belief systems we have about ourselves, who we are, who we are not and what we are capable of. Every thing, every person, every object becomes a physical expression of ourselves, and it either represents our fears, our lack, our self respect and much more. We then realize that those things are not truly creating joy, peace or fulfillment in the way that we thought they were supposed to... and so it begins: the dissolution of your entire reality. It can start with as simple as the letting go of some of these material accumulations, years and years of books, notebooks, greeting cards received, old photographs, old letters, pictures, albums, CDs, and the list goes on and on. There is a moment where you realize everything is truly just taking up space for the things that you now know truly support you. Of course, some of things take time, sometimes years, to let go of, for there is so much emotional attachment to some of them that until you allow yourself to feel every emotion attached to that memory or to that thing, then and only then will your whole entire being be ready to release that object. Other times it is easy and effortlessly, sometimes you force yourself to just let it all go, sometimes you have to talk yourself into doing it and remind yourself that if you were to ever need this again somehow the frequency of it will make its way back into your life. In the end, it isn't truly the object that matters but the energy, the frequency or the feeling that that object represents, or that it holds. This makes it a lot easier to actually let go of so much stuff that is no longer needed in one's life. This may feel like a small step or a small start but it is a huge part of the process. The physical dissolution of the material things that are keeping us bound to old realities is MONUMENTAL, and you may not start to fully see it or feel it until things start to change in your world.

Think or feel all of those things that we kept for years and years in our reality, your body has to hold all of that stuff in place because that is just how things work. Every physical and non-physical thing, experience and memory is held by a gridding system that we hold in place through the muscles in our body. As you start to purge more and more physical things from your reality your physical/body structure will start to dissolve an enormous amount of heaviness that was anchored inside. It can get much more intricate and fascinating but to put it simple terms everything that you have in your environment/reality is literally held up by your physical body. Once something is moved, shifted, and/or completely removed the entire gridding system of your body shifts and morphs in ways that you will start to feel and inner-stand the more you open up to it.

This becomes a truly fascinating experience the more you embrace it.

The Linear Mind

With any of these processes that I've mentioned or that you've heard about or even engaged in yourself there is something very important to remember and that is the linear mind will take it, run with it and make it something that it is not. The ego mind latches on to the idea that things need to be intricate, complicated, hard and challenging in order to prove something to someone. This is where we get caught up in a loop cycle in which the mind tries to do everything, resolve everything, dissolve everything but yet it keeps creating more and more stories, emotional turmoil and upheaval that keeps this alive. Things are actually much simpler than the mind can perceive.

The dissolution, even clearing and transmuting and so many other processes that assist in our expansion is something that we also need to surrender and trust fully and completely. Our Light/LightBody is meant to take over for it knows exactly what to do at a deeper, cellular and DNA level. It's almost like the linear mind doesn't have access to these areas until we evolve and activate our Higher Mind Consciousness in which that is a whole other experience within itself. In the meantime we must learn to regain trust back on our Light, our LightBodies, our higher hearts instead of fixating to the idea that our linear minds have to know and do everything. This elongates and prolongs a process that is not actually that complicated. Once you surrender and allow your Light to take over in every way you will start to see how much simple things are. This is where our ego constructs must be seen, recognized, acknowledged and allowed back into our hearts so that they don't get in the way anymore.

You don't have to know every single thing that occurs in the dissolution process, you don't have to understand it all fully, you just have to allow it to unfold and let your whole body/being be immersed in the experience as its highest aligned and when you are guided to do something that will assist it then you follow the guidance and do it. It's almost like becoming that pure, innocent child again that is fully trusting of its Light and follows the commands it is told because it knows that it will make things easier and smoother if it does. It's only when our separated aspects of ourselves that are still angry, hurt, rebellious inside that things become hard. When this occurs now that you are battling an aspect of yourself that has unresolved issues that must be resolved or that aspect will make it impossible to move forward.

Again this is a big part of the process, dissolving all aspects of ourselves back into the purity of heart. There are countless ways to do this, there is not one way and one way alone for each aspect is different and each aspect that you work with may need different things at different times and this is where being fully present in that moment and communicating with this aspect is key because it will lead you to exactly what he/she needs/wants in order to open up fully and return home.

The most important thing to remember is that the deeper you connect inside, the more present and open you become in every moment no matter what the circumstance may be and therefore the easier it will be for you to know what is needed in that moment.

As you begin to trust, listen and surrender the guidance will come and your Light will be able to resolve and dissolve everything back to Light again without it being a complicated endeavor. The more you relax into your body, relax your mind and being the easier it is for your Light to work through and bring you back to pure peace and balance inside.

FEEL/SENSE

As Light Beings in a physical body we automatically come with an emotional/sensory mechanism that allows us to feel/sense/perceive in a way that uniquely characterizes the human experience/experiment. The sensory receptors have been programmed in a way that only allows a limited perception of the greater scheme of the entire human reality but needless to say it is part of how we created the 3D system. As sentient beings we have the capacity to feel things beyond the five senses and beyond our linear minds but this is only possible when we allow ourselves to go past the perceived limitations and activate every system/organ/cell/DNA within our physical structure. It is in this continual activation that we are able to expand our consciousness and our perception in a way that fully supports our LightBody/Soul/Light in every capacity. The lower/physical realms of this reality can only perceive things based on the five sensory constructs and even then we don't fully utilize them.

As you allow to fully engage all of your senses in every experience you'll start to open up the receptors and you'll be able to perceive and receive more information/guidance from that said experience. The more open you are to every experience the more open you are to higher levels of consciousness that will bring forth more awareness as to why you are creating the experience, what is creating the experience, what is feeding this experience and much more. If the experience is less than pure then you have the ability to shift/re-aling and recreate a whole new experience that is fully aligned with peace and love.

Being Present

One of the most important aspects to recognize is that when we are playing out a human reality that is less than peaceful, pure or loving it that it is being created mostly unconsciously because we aren't truly being completely present. We live in either the past or the future but rarely from the sacredness of the present moment. We have a misperception that where we are, what we have and who we are is just not enough and so we have to keep reaching, keep pulling, keep desiring something else that is perceived to be better than what's here and now.

This mentality/program keeps us bound to the "future" and anchored in the "past" without fully engaging and enjoying the now experience. When one is not fully present then all the senses aren't fully engaged in the experience and this is integral for one to be able to not just be open and receptive but actually enjoy the entire reality. This has kept us closed off, guarded and scared of possibly feeling/realizing something that we may believe we are not ready for. Let's dive deeper.

During this life/existence there are moments/experiences/people that trigger off an emotion or memory that is connected to a time in the perceived past that was not loving, peaceful or joyful. This causes a deeply embedded protection/survival mechanism that has been intrinsically put in place in our physical body/field to activate/go off. When these receptors are triggered one is actually brought back into that experience and "logically" speaking the human mind does not want to repeat that experience therefore it suppresses the emotion and escapes, keeping itself from feeling or being in the present moment.

However when one keeps suppressing and escaping from every experience that bring forth these emotions the emotional heaviness only keeps getting bigger and heavier. The body starts to feel the heaviness and toxicity of all suppressed emotions and starts to acquire many imbalances that may cause sickness, dis-ease, or chronic things.

The linear/human/logic mind will continue to not want to feel because it is scared of feeling, scared of recreating that same scenario, scared of being free, scared of judgment and so much more. The Higher Mind however is connected to the Higher Heart and perceives the opposite of the linear mind. It remembers how much it's loved, wanted and supported and therefore it is more open to allowing all the emotions to come up to feel them fully.

As you allow yourself to be fully present in each moment, you become more open to every experience no matter what it may bring forth. The Higher Mind/Heart remembers that there is so much freedom in being fully open, fully aware and conscious of every experience. This aspect of yourself is not afraid of the emotion and so it embraces it.

The power of being present in each moment is that one actually starts to dissolve the fear of the present, fear of feeling, fear of recreating a hurtful experience because it knows that fear is just an illusion and when one keeps on believing in it we just keep creating more of it. When you allow yourself to sit with the feeling, be fully present with it there is a magical biochemical/alchemical/energetic reaction that the body goes through in which it releases the discord and disharmony that was held in place by that emotion.

One doesn't have to understand it fully it just needs to be in full trust and surrender that the body/LightBody knows exactly what to do to restore the body back to pure peace and balance.

Feeling Fully

There is much that gets triggered in the body when one starts to feel a heavy emotion. Not to mention that the way we've programmed this reality is one where we are not accepting of certain emotions. Yes, we created a mentality that perceived it is not safe to cry, it is not good to show anger, it is not right to be emotional; emotions and showing emotions is shown as weak, vulnerable, unmanly and in a way even inhuman when it is nothing but the completely opposite. We are sentient beings and therefore it is normal to be emotional, feel our emotions, release our emotions so we are not controlled by them AND so we don't keep creating experiences that will keep triggering them.

Emotions are a huge part of the process and because we've suppressed so many of them throughout every single one of our existences and previous timelines then it is only normal that as we navigate the ascension journey/4D realm that we are going to be confronted by every single one of them so we can fully feel them, embrace them and release them from the physical body.

Every emotion is just a frequency, it doesn't have an identity per say, we are the ones that have labeled emotions as good/bad, right/wrong, positive/negative, when this creates more judgment about them inside. When you start to dissolve all the labels, identities, judgments, beliefs that one still carries inside about emotions one is able to free itself and no longer judge oneself for feeling a certain way. Emotions are just a way for us to put words to something we are feeling inside. It is a way to describe what's going on inside and a clue/sign that can also assist us in recognizing where are we functioning from and what we have yet to resolve inside from a younger age. Emotions become a very integral part of our reality that assists us instead of something that oppresses us or something we have to fear. Our entire perception changes when we open up to them and embrace their true role in this reality.

Sensory Perception

The senses of the body hold much more information than the linear/human mind can perceive. Every sense in the body is connected and wired in a way that assist the human body when we open ourselves to this new program. Yes, the old program which is now becoming obsolete, was wired in a way that was quite detrimental to the human body and to our Light and this is partly because of how the DNA was programmed to begin with. The sensory receptors were programmed just as the 3D matrix program was, deeply embedded in fear, lack, judgment, shame and much more. This created a lot of separation inside that didn't allow us to fully express ourselves as Light, it didn't allow us to hear our guidance, hear the supportive frequencies of nature and Gaia, it didn't allow us to stop and smell the flowers, it didn't allow us to see all that truly supports us, it didn't allow us to trust our gut feelings, our inner knowing, our heart and so much more. It's almost like we've had all of these receptors blocked or infiltrated by the old systems and structures that kept feeding us things/sounds/smells/foods/etc that kept us dormant, unconscious and scared shitless. Now this is all part of how we programmed this reality to be and we did this for many reasons. However now as many people are waking up and remembering we are starting to see things differently, our perceptions are starting to open up and change, which means our senses are starting to smell how rotten things have actually been in this unconscious reality.

Our senses are now becoming our truth detectors; they are supporting us in giving us messages that support our journey and our LightBody more than ever before. One of the many things that have blocked our sensory receptors is our emotions. Our emotions have caused much turmoil and heaviness inside of the body which also create a deeply rooted system that separates and disconnects all of our senses, organs, cells and much more. As we each start to open up to our emotions and feel them fully we will start to open up these receptors more and more and connect them back to our Higher Heart and Mind in the most powerful ways yet. This is about going all in with each heavy emotion that comes through for you. Anytime you feel something heavy that needs to be felt and embraced, get your body to fully feel it. It's not just a cry until your cry your eyes out, this is a cry not just with your eyes but with your entire body. Every cell, atom, muscle, bone in your body has been carrying that emotional frequency for too long and so as you allow yourself to engage fully with every part, every muscle and every fiber of your being you'll start to release it fully from the physical body and also from all other energy bodies as well. This is a massive and so powerful release that needs to occur in every level because of how intrinsic and complex and subconscious the emotional frequency has been anchored into the body to keep one in the lower realms. Like previously mentioned the body knows exactly what to do if we just support it by going all in without judgement. This becomes a much simpler and beautiful process than one we thought.

When you allow your full LightBody to take over you will start to feel a recalibration, recoding and rebalancing that restores back pure peace and purity so deep inside that you knew you wouldn't have been able to achieve from your linear mind. This is why it's crucial to start fully allowing and surrendering more and more deeper and deeper to your Light/Soul/LightBody in every way and when you do you will start to feel how loved and supported you are in this entire process and journey, way more than you believe.

EMBRACE

Our misperceptions and judgments have blocked us from expanded and Higher levels of consciousness. A lot of the times we create so much judgment towards ourselves based on the perceived notion of what we should be, how we should act, what we should be/do/say, and so we carry this judgment and apply it to everything we perceive to be "outside" of ourselves. Anything and everything that doesn't fit in the old boxes, doesn't conform to the old ways, anything that doesn't make linear sense is not embraced, accepted or wanted. This has caused much pain and suffering in our world in a myriad of ways far too vast and complex to fully share here but I know you can feel this.

When we can't accept, embrace and honor exactly who we are and what is going on with our realities, our LightBodies, our world then we are creating a frequency of resistance, fear, judgment and lack/not good enough. Our bodies and our physical realities are undergoing an enormous amount of shifts and changes in a very short amount of time and this is all happening for a reason. Our Soul knows more than our Human mind can comprehend at this time and it is time to reconnect with it at all costs and in all levels so we can start to fully honor, accept and embrace what is actually going on.

The frequencies of this planet are rising to a level and degree in which it allows more Light to come through for all of the inhabitants living on it at this time. The Light coming through at this time is significantly higher than it's ever been for quite some time and it is increasing by the minute. This will continue to create a reality in which more and more people continue to wake up, continue to remember and see beyond the perceived illusion also called the veils of amnesia by many. This also raises the consciousness of all which allows a deeper level of innerstanding of all that has transpired on this planet. The higher levels of consciousness humans have the more connected they will become to themselves and with everything around them which will create a unified existence that will support all beings in every way. The level of separation that humans have perceived up until this point has disconnected them from the sacredness of who they are and the sacredness that all is at a deep level and therefore they have been able to live/exist/perform things in a way that has detrimentally affected the entire collective and planet in more ways than we can comprehend at this time. It is up to each and every single person on this planet to choose differently and this comes forth by raising the level of consciousness that each person holds inside of their own body.

The process of ascending an entire planet and collective is extremely complex and intricate and everyone that incarnated here during this time knew exactly that this would occur during this exact time in history. Many have already chosen whether to physical ascend in this incarnation or not, others have agreed at a Soul level to only assist for a brief period of time until they choose to leave their physical body and continue somewhere else. This is just part of the ascension process that we must all learn to embrace as each Soul is consciously assisting and supporting this process in more ways than our linear minds can comprehend.

Every event, every perceived catastrophe, every collapse, every change, every mandate, every reality is supporting the entire process at some level from a different dimensional reality. Every person, every animal, every being, every aspect, every relationship, every reality that is being presented in eachs world is also supporting each in waking/remembering/activating deeper levels of their Soul remembrance. Every person is being shaken up and shown new things that will create a powerful force within for them to open up their hearts/minds/bodies more and more so they can start to perceive things differently. Yes, it all boils down to perception and how one CHOOSES to see things, not what others want you to see and not allowing other peoples' lens to influence your own inner vision that will/can reflect a different reality than the one being shown to the masses. Each person will need to tune deeper inside and start to see/feel from the lens of their pure heart and inner vision instead of from the television. This will greatly change our own perception of what all is and what all is doing and as each opens their Higher Heart more and more and more one will start to remember that all is happening for a higher purpose and the greater good of this massive ascension process that all is a part of whether they are conscious of it or not, that does not matter at all.

The Higher Heart and Mind will become the way in which we are able to shift our perceptions and perspectives of all. We will be able to remember that as a Soul we don't ever fully die because death is a construct that was build on fear and lack and that was tightly kept in place by the 3D matrix system. The polarity of things being "terrible", "horrible," "good/bad," "right/wrong" are also structures build in place that only exist in the 3D world of duality in which things can only be perceived from a very limited and constricted view. The higher you raise your frequency, the more expanded your state of consciousness becomes and the more you're able to remember that these concepts simply don't exist in the Unified Field of Consciousness which is who all are at deep sacred level. Therefore everything that happens in the old 3D world is only a fraction of all that is truly going on and as we open up more to see more we start to feel/sense/know that everything is supporting the ascension process of humanity. The end of the 3D conscious world is happening and it is going to be up to each and every single one of us to leave that reality and open up completely to experience the beauty and magic of the 5D+/New Earth/Paradise that already exists on Gaia. The more we each open up to the idea that this world already exists and continuously hold the vibrational frequency of it in every way and in every moment then and only then will we start to perceive and experience it.

Open up to embrace that things are actually happening for you, to support the massive clearing and expansion of your heart/body/mind instead of the opposite limited view that things are happening to you from a victim mentality. Open up to remembering that everything that is happening is gifting you the opportunity to actually becoming more in tuned with your body, with who you are and who you came here to be. Open up to the idea that every experience and reality right now is opening up new doors of opportunities and possibilities that at one time you didn't even dream they were possible. Open up to the idea that everything right now is bringing forth so much Light to assist you in seeing more, feeling more, becoming more, allowing more and achieving more from a state of purity inside instead of from the old ego constructs and separation mentalities that only created more fear, lack and judgement. Open up and dare to be free of the old ideas and limitations, control and manipulation that only keep you in boxes believing that you are small, frail, weak, fragile, powerless, dumb, stupid, incapable, unworthy and so many other things that we accepted as true. Open up to all that is coming forth for you and all the liberation that is happening at a deep cellular/DNA level that we may not see with our own physical eyes yet but we can start to feel/sense/know the more we open up to it and just embrace it all.

Keep opening up and embracing it all because the more you do the more you'll start to experience a completely new, different, vibrant and amazing reality that supports your entire body/Soul/Light in ways that were not possible in the old 3D conscious reality.

ACCEPT

There is so much magic in learning to accept, accepting where one is, accepting all that is happening, accepting ones feelings, accepting all that one is and has been. We have this perception that we should only accept one reality, one perception, one truth when there is so much more to everything that is going on in every moment. When one can't accept, one is in resistance; it is blocking the door that holds much wisdom and knowledge on the other side. When something is not going the way that we want it to go, or think it should go or desire it to go a lot of the time we are not willing to accept it, we are not willing to come to terms with it and instead we fight it, we turn away from it, we disown it and we push/pull/fight/work so hard to change it. There is nothing wrong with shifting/re-creating something because we are Source Creator Beings and as such we are always creating our reality but the intention behind it makes a HUGE different.

What's the Intention?

In this fast-paced world/society where we are rarely sitting still and/or fully present, we are constantly creating a reality from an unconscious/closed space. We don't know why things happen, we don't remember that we are creating our entire world let alone how to change it. In this unconscious state we aren't able to fully appreciate everything that is going on because we live in a state of deep amnesia. As we start to wake up and remember that there is more to life, more to us, more to this world and more to what we are capable of, things start to change. The more conscious we become and the more we start to remember who we are at our core and what that entails we start to see how everything around us is created through the energy we hold, our deeply anchored thoughts, our emotions, our beliefs, our words, our choices, our thoughts, our environment and so much more. Each of these holds a very important part of the creation puzzle and it is up to us to start to identify what puzzle pieces are creating our physical reality.

Throughout this journey we start to remember that as Creator Beings we are creating every experience and as such we start to take full responsibility of it. Yes, our ego loves to play in victimhood, because it is easier to point fingers and not be accountable, it is easier to just wait for others to change and keep being/doing the same old things, it is easier to keep hiding, playing small, going with the old identities and belief systems. Of course, "easy" is only a perception because in the long run, it only creates more pain, suffering, fear and lack. The more one keeps playing this game the harder it is for the body to function, and therefore the harder it is for our Soul/Light to come through and the less Light one holds inside of the body the harder it is for the body to sustain itself.

Being fully accepting of one's creation takes time, in fact it is a process. We start to process little bits of information that gives us clues as to how we created our reality. At first, we start to see how our words and thoughts start to materialize in many different ways throughout our day; we start to see all sorts of synchronicities, repeating numbers, messages and other things that go far beyond the linear/logical mind. We start to open up to a new way of seeing things, a new belief system that isn't taught in school, we start to break free from the norm and our mind begins to stretch a little more and a little more and a little more.

Some of us were introduced to books or movies like The Secret, or the Law of Attraction. Others go more into the metaphysical route, spirituality, energy and the like, and each are very supportive in the expansion of consciousness. Thinking outside of the box, asking more questions, becoming more curious about how this world actually works are all steps that we all take; they allow more knowledge to come through in our reality. Like previously mentioned, some of it takes a while to process and some of it feels so true inside that you don't even question it, it's something engrained in your very core that you just know it's true.

As you being to open up more of your mind/heart/body you start to remember far more than what your human memory holds, you start to tap into your cellular memory, your Heart's inner knowing and your DNA knowledge that goes far beyond the logical/linear truth. This is a normal and very important part of one's phase and journey because we all have to be open to the crazy, the bizarre and all that makes no logical sense, doesn't fit into the normal societal boxes of truth, religion and sometimes even science. We must be willing to be the crazy ones that no longer take what at face value what is still taught and preached in the old world and dare to go above and beyond the limitations of the mind. This world is far more complex, intricate and more magical than we could ever imagine and we are finally breaking free from the old ways so we can start to access all the infinite and limitless possibilities that actually exist.

Each and every person will have to choose this for themselves, we as WayShowers can only guide and support as it's appropriate and aligned. We share the keys and codes to assist those that are ready and open for more.

As you start to open up to more of what's already inside of you, you will become more aware of all the intentions that are active in your inner world that are creating your physical reality. Yes, there are many things playing out inside of you that most of the time we have no clue of. There are many beliefs, emotions, thoughts, thought forms, existences that are simultaneously being played out in every moment and that are transmitting the frequencies and codes that are bringing forth a reality that matches the exact same frequencies and codes. Simply put, you create what you believe and allow, meaning all your deepest, most imbedded belief systems that you consciously, unconsciously and subconsciously hold in your body/field are creating the tones that are then transmitted out for your reality to form. Of course there is more to this but I'm keeping things simple.

When we start to slow down, become more present with our thoughts, our words, our actions we can start to become more aware of what is behind everything. Our true intentions start to be seen more, perceived more and the more we can see them the more we will start to recognize where we are coming from. We need to become so fully aware of what is the motive of our actions, why are we really saying those words, why do we want that those things, why do feel we need this or that because the more we start to recognize the intention we will start becoming more aware of the deeper questions of why do we keep creating this in our reality, why do we keep attracting these relationships, why do we keep going back to these habits, why we keep going through these cycles, and so on. This becomes necessary in order for each one of us to actually do something that completely changes and shifts the outcome of anything. Instead of continuing to play out the same old cycles, playing the same old records, cremating the same results, when we know our true motives and core intentions we will finally start to see the root of all and as a result we can start to make powerful changes.

Open Up

Opening up to seeing and accepting all that you have within you is a massive undertaking but it is necessary in order to start embodying who we are as Source Creator Beings. As you start to dive deeper within, you will start to see many things, some things are easier to take in than others and that's normal, it's part of the journey of re-discovering yourself. We are all going to have to come to terms with some things that are harsh, rough, tough, painful and very emotional but it is in seeing it all, feeling it all, accepting it all then one can find true freedom inside. If we keep suppressing or denying it, it will only keep getting bigger and bigger and much heavier than before. It isn't until you fully allow yourself to expand past your perception of what this energy should be, should look or should feel that we start to not hold on to it. When you just see things for what they are, without labeling them, or judging them, or trying to fix or change what you see you allow every energy/frequency/aspect/structure/belief system tied to it to shift in the most magical and powerful way. Our heart opens, our body opens, our field opens and everything starts to re-align without you having to do anything but just be with it in this sacred space of acceptance.

Our minds are the ones that get in the way, they are the ones that want to fix things, or want to push things away because it perceived things as being wrong, bad, evil or sinful; all that is just tied to the old limited perceptions of how things actually are. Things are never cut and dry, black and white, good or bad and if we keep labeling them as such, our judgement of them will keep things locked up inside of us. This old fixated way will just continue to recreate more harsh circumstances/experiences that will break us open so we can finally remember/see the purpose of it. The energy that we truly are as Light Beings is so powerful, pure and so infinite; it embraces us, accepts all, loves all because it remembers that all is energy and all is just a reflection of itself and therefore at the core of it all it is Love.

We are all remembering this and we are starting to come back to existing as Unity Consciousness and through that remembrance we allow everything to just be. Just by us showing love and appreciation and pure acceptance of what all is we literally create a force that unwinds, rewinds, rewrites everything back to its pure, organic nature. Yes, it's that simple and the more we allow it to be so the more all shift back into Unity.

You don't have to fully inner-stand, comprehend or even believe it at the beginning because it does feel like it's way out there from what we've been taught, you just have to begin to open up a little bit more and a little bit more and as you do our heart/mind/body/field will start to unlock all the Divine inner knowing that you already hold inside that will assist you in expanding your consciousness and remember all the things that at a core level you already know.

Accepting Our Most Wounded and Distorted Aspects

It is in becoming accepting of all that we are/have been/perceived to be that we start to find a deeper sense of peace. Ever since I went all in on my ascension process I started recognizing aspects of myself that I had no idea I had. These were versions of myself that I had never or rarely connected with, they were the angriest aspects of myself, the ones that had been the most suppressed inside that they were literally the opposite of who I've been in this existence. I innately started to offer them a space in which they could be, say, express what they truly thought and felt about anything and everything that was going on in my current reality. At first it was quite interesting and shocking at the same time because the things that came out wasn't what or how I would normally express myself but I knew there had to be something to this.

I started to realize and remember more and more and everything started to make more sense. The versions of ourselves that are the most deeply suppressed are the ones that are miles apart from the character we've played most of our lives or at least far from the one we've allowed ourselves to be. Most of the time the people we come to dislike, disgust and/or judge have characteristics that are very similar to these aspects which is why we choose people in our reality to be that because we cannot see those aspects within ourselves. In fact everyone that is perceived to be outside of ourselves is actually a mere reflection of an aspect we still hold inside. Many of these aspects are those that are still separated from love, are very hurt, angry and sad and because we don't want to feel this way or come to terms with the fact that we have these emotions inside we suppress the very thought of it all. When we do this the only way for us to see what's deeply suppressed is for us to see it in our "external" reality being played by someone else. This is one of the many reasons why when we cast judgment upon others, when we blame and point fingers, when we are disrespectful and hurtful towards others in reality we are only doing it to ourselves because "they" are us.

When we open up to feeling all that we have inside everything starts to change. Not only that but as we allow ourselves to see every aspect of ourselves exactly for what it is, what it's feeling, what it wants to say, what it wants to do it brings an enormous amount of freedom to this aspect and to ourselves. Underneath it all everyone has unresolved emotions, wounded aspects and unhealed experiences including our own aspects. Underneath it all there is small, scared to death child that only wants to be loved and accepted, heard and supported, valued and respected no matter what. Many of us are too quick to judge and too slow to forgive and all this really does is slow down our own completion process and prolongs our path to inner freedom. As silly as this may sound we have many aspects inside that are scared to be free, are scared to be loved and supported and many times because of an old perception of what they think that actually means.

It is up to each and every single one of us to start giving ourselves permission to be with every part of ourselves, no matter how ugly, evil, distorted, hurtful and hateful that part of us feels like. This isn't truly who we are but it is still someone we chose to be and for that we just give it our space and time as a way of showing love for ourselves so that we no longer have aspects of ourselves that are unwhole and separated.

This is a continual process that becomes a normal part of the journey in which we all just embrace and honor. It does become easier and easier because the more Light we hold inside the less resistant we are to the entire process. Open yourself up fully and become the observer, the pure love Being that you truly are and as you do the more whole and complete you become in every way and across all existences.

OPEN

This whole existence and journey is about being opening, staying opening and keep opening up; it sounds so simple but yet it is one of the most challenging things to do. Being open is about opening up your entire mind, body, heart and Soul and this is exactly what we've been taught not to do. We have been taught that keeping ourselves small, quiet, hidden and protected is safer than being fully open and vulnerable, therefore being open feels very threatening, unprotected and dangerous. Being open to change and to new ideas goes against everything we've been taught and it is embedded deep in our subconscious. Most of us for much of our lives run around in fear, locked up and hidden, suppressing our emotions and feelings and this creates a reality that is less than joyful and peaceful. It creates an identity in which we pretend to be ok, we pretended to live happy and fulfilled lives when in reality it's quite the opposite.

From the time we were toddlers we've been told the word "No" far too many times than we can count. And it's not that the word no shouldn't be said but the context in which this word is used is based on fear. It perpetuates the idea that one should always be fearful of our actions and therefore one must be still, silent and paralyzed. The entire structure of our 3D reality is literally based on this concept, it is based on fear and lack, it is created on limitations and rules that say "don't do that, don't say that, don't think that" and so on and so forth. Again this keeps us closed and separated from who we are at our core.

Separation is the core root of fear and lack, it is the feeling of being separated and alone that creates a chemical imbalance in our bodies, it is what creates an illusion in the mind that we aren't loved and supported, it is literally the opposite of who we are and of how things are. Being and keeping ourselves closed off perpetuates this feeling of separation that keeps us so far from our essence, it separates us from one another and it activates much chaos in our world.

Thing of being in a house, where everyone kept their doors closed, everyone kept to themselves, everyone locked themselves inside of their room and rarely came out. No one really talks to each other because of fear, no one is there for each other because they are deaf to each other, no one hugs one another for fear they might attract an illness, no one sees, hears, feels or senses each other because everyone has kept themselves so closed off that it numbs the very essence of who we are. This goes so far that the people in this house are even blind and deaf to themselves, they can't hear themselves, they don't know what they need, they don't know what they want, they can't feel anything and their very existence is a very cold and linear one that completely shuts off their own Light.

This is basically what many of us have lived and experienced at some level throughout many existences; many of us without even knowing or even sensing that this is what is actually happening. We've been running around our lives so shut off and closed off from everything and everyone that we have consciously and unconsciously been carrying around all of our hurt, all of our anger, all of our grief, our despair, our sadness and every emotion known to man. This is what happens when we keep ourselves so closed off that we don't even allow ourselves to feel our own emotions and we just keep stuffing them deeper and deeper inside so that we don't see them, so that others don't notice them, so that we don't have to deal with them and feel them. When all of our doors and windows are so locked up and closed then we don't give ourselves permission to feel, we don't give ourselves the opportunity to be free from all of the emotional baggage that we've been carrying for years. It's like carrying around with you every bag of trash that you have accumulated since you were born... just imagine living in a space, in a house where you have trash everywhere, bags and bags of garbage that just sit and pile up day after day and although it is uncomfortable to live this way, you've accepted it, you've acclimated to it, you've numbed your entire body that you can't even see or smell anything at all.

This has been us. This has been our reality for far too long and finally we are being blessed with the opportunity that allows us to feel this, we are starting to sense just how crazy it is to be so locked up and closed that we don't even take our own trash out. All our emotions have been piling and piling up and we are finally starting to feel the heaviness of it all, our bodies are starting to wake up and feel this, our nervous systems are finally getting so triggered that all our fears and worries are coming up to the surface for us to see, our digestive system is becoming so unsettled that we are beginning to purge all of our unresolved, unfelt, undigested emotions.... And so much more is happening.

We are starting to open up. We are starting to value ourselves, value our bodies, value our emotions, value our feelings, value our freedom. We are finally starting to choose to no longer carry the weight of our fears, our lack, our worries on our bodies. We are choosing to open up our doors, windows and see ourselves, see one another, see the backwards reality in which we lived in for so long. We are starting to break free from the old and it all starts with being open.

Our Essence

Being open and expansive is who we truly are. This is what we are as Light, as pure Beings, as Soul Beings. When we incarnated on this planet in this human body, we feel the separation so tangibly that we believe it. We absorbed everything around us that says we are small, weak and separated from everything and everyone. We acquire the constructs of the linear mind that keeps us in fear and lack and we begin to mold into what society believes we should be. This is part of just how the 3D world operates, it is how we created this reality and it is why we came here, to change it back to its pure original state.

We are shifting and evolving ourselves out of our own separation. We are dissolving everything inside that keeps us closed and separated by feeling everything, honoring everything and respecting every person, every reality, every experience and every creation. We are starting to remember that everything has a higher role and higher purpose and it is only when we start to fully focus on ourselves, our bodies, our emotions, our thoughts that everything around us starts to change as well. We have to be willing to open up our eyes, open up our mind and open up our hearts to becoming aware of everything that is going on in our own world and how it is just a mere reflection of our internal world. We were so closed and shut off from everything that we forgot just how this world works, we forgot that everything perceive to be "outside" is deeply connected to all we still have inside; our unresolved issues, unfelt emotions, unworthy self perceptions are all coming up to the surface in a way that we can't discount them anymore, we can't hide from them and we cannot deny them any longer. There is simply no other way around it, we have to be willing to see and feel everything because then and only then will we start to fully inner-stand the purpose of why we created it in the first place.

As we begin to remember and inner-stand the inner workings of our mind and body then we start to appreciate they for what they are trying to tell us and we start to become more conscious of the choices and decisions that perpetuated those circumstances.

Opening up our Heart

There is an old belief that says we must guard ourselves, protect our heart so that we don't get hurt again. It is as if the heart was small, weak and powerless; we hold on to this belief so tightly that we forget what pure love is, we forget how to love not just others but ourselves and we let the fear and protection mechanisms rule our entire reality.

We have kept our hearts closed believing that it would keep us safe when in reality that has only kept us more separated from our pure essence. The safety and protection mechanisms are based on the idea and belief that something outside of yourself is more powerful, stronger, and that it's sole intention is to harm you. When we are closed off from who we are, yes everything seems bigger than us, stronger than us and in that same reality we keep ourselves small and hidden because we fear that if we are big and seen then we are at risk. This is a subconscious belief that has been passed down for many generations and that has been following us for many existences and it perpetuates the aspect of us that feels and believes in separation so strongly that it holds on to it as if it's own life depended on it.

We have kept our hearts closed because we are afraid to feel everything that is deep down inside of us. We perceive that feeling makes us weak and vulnerable when in truth it makes us real and open. Our emotions shouldn't be something we fear but rather something we embrace because no matter how heavy they are at times, no matter how painful they might seem, they are the bridge that connects us to our Soul, our Heart and our Light. It is through our emotions that we dissolve the separation we hold inside and we start to feel the purity that we are. Our emotions are safe, our emotions are part of this human experience, they aren't something to suppress, hide, fear, disown or be ashamed of for each and every single person is bound to feel them... it is simply how the human body functions, it is part of the chemistry that we have and as such it should be accepted. Our emotions are a way in which the body communicates to us, they are here to teach us about ourselves and even though the heavy emotions are the hardest and most challenging to deal with they are the most important ones to honor because they hold the key to everything.

The heavy emotions are the ones we are most afraid to feel, they are the ones attached to stories and experiences that created much pain, suffering and separated us so much from our pure essence that we believe that if we were to feel them all over again we would re-create that unwanted experience and get stuck in it. If I can offer you another perspective, one that frees you from this belief so that you can free yourself of the emotional attachment that you have is this, when you give yourself permission to feel even the most heaviest and painful of these heavy emotions with your entire body, mind and heart, something magical occurs... you surrender... you stop holding on to it.. you let go.. you begin to relax into a state where you're no longer fighting with this emotion. Your whole entire body, begins to breathe, it opens up, it allows more Light to come through and as this happens light codes start coming in to do the heavy duty lifting, the cellular cleansing, the DNA activation, the molecular restructuring and so much more. The key is to feel the emotion with your entire body, with every cell, with all that you are, not just with your mind. Many of us feel the emotion by just crying and yet from my experience sometimes this isn't enough, your entire body has to fully feel it in order to fully release it. It's a process, and it make take practice because we've been so disconnected from our bodies that we may not even fully know what it's like to feel with our bodies... yes, our entire bodies have been shut down and numbed in many ways and the suppression of our emotions is just but one of them.

I challenge you to open up completely to every emotion that comes up for you, open up to all that you're feeling, give yourself permission to feel it all no matter what it is and no matter how heavy it is. It is in those moments where I have allowed myself to feel the deeper, heaviest, most suppressed emotions that I had no idea I had that I declared myself free and sovereign from them, it's like your whole body screams a plea and declares to honor it for what it is and at the same time chooses to no longer be enslaved by it. It is one of the most powerful experiences for sure and feeling all that emotional pain makes it all worthwhile in the end.

Don't think too much about it, just let your whole entire body surrender fully to the experience and you'll start to feel the freedom that it will bring forth.

PURIFY

    There is a purification process that takes place in every level of your being: emotional, mental, spiritual, physical and even beyond that. When we come down into this body, the carbon-based structure allows for much baggage to get stored inside and as you begin to consciously or unconsciously open up you start to get rid of this baggage which simultaneously creates an alchemical reaction in the body that allows a purification of everything. In one aspect the LightBody does the purification of each cell, muscle, organ inside of the body and one must fully surrender to it and in another aspect one must start to consciously start to purify and cleanse everything in their own physical reality. This is where the physical purging becomes a very important part of the process; everything that is tied to an old reality, an old version of yourself, an old emotional experience has to be completely and fully released in every level. In many cases the physical detachment serves in freeing the entire body from it. The less the body is attached to a physical object, emotion, experience or person the more expansive the body becomes and the more space one creates inside for the Light of your Soul to live in your body.

    The cellular purification process is intricate and complex and this is why we let the LightBody handle this part; in the macro level it is simple, all we have to do is re-align everything in our reality that allows the space and energy for our pure Light to come through in every aspect of our being and in every part of our reality. There is a very important part of the process where we come to have very little material things, we come to embrace and honor our space in a way that we have no need to accumulate things in a way that it will inter-fear with our mind, body and Soul. Yes, we become very "picky" in a sense about what we allow into our reality and who we allow as well; we become very sensitive in a way that allows us to feel what is aligned and what is not aligned with our Soul. Everything becomes a very important piece of our reality and we become very conscious of everything as well.

Purifying Our Words, Thoughts and Actions

Sometimes when we think of the word purify we perceive that to mean that things were "dirty", "polluted", "not clean", among other things and in a way it is true. Our Higher self aspect and Soul are very pure but our ego/separated aspects are quite the opposite. These aspects are separated, distorted, backwards and heavy. They are tied to a reality that created a world that has no respect and honor for the energy that resides on this planet and therefore created a "dirty, polluted, unclean" reality that can be physically seen.

This is connected to the mentality and state of consciousness that one operates from. The more one believes and operates from a state of separation, the more disconnected one is from themselves and therefore the entire world; this leads to us engaging in actions, behaviors that are detrimental to the society as a whole. This is when people live their lives completely disconnected from their actions and completely oblivious to the fact that their choices affect others around them. It isn't until one starts to open up and become more conscious that words, thoughts, behaviors, actions do influence others and the planet we start to change things.

Our words matter, our thoughts matter, our actions matter way more than our linear minds can comprehend. The more we open up and start to see how much these things affect our reality the more we start to change them. The energy of our words, thoughts and actions lead to a mentality, which lead to a belief system, which lead to the structures that create our entire physical reality. The key is to not control them but become aware of what it is that we are saying, thinking and doing and what the intention is behind it all.

Many of us still fall under the presumption that we need to change these things by simply controlling, suppressing and denying them. This isn't about any of this at all; this is about fully honoring everything in a way that frees you from the energy. Words, thoughts and actions are simply energy, they have a signature, they can be used to create or destroy and it's important to recognize what you are creating and what you are destroying. We came here to create a New Earth reality and destroy/collapse the old earth reality. Every word either supports New Earth or supports old earth, same thing with your thoughts and actions; they are either tied to New Earth or keep you bound to old earth. The challenge is to be open enough to honor everything that flows from you because as energy it needs an outlet, it needs you to open up to it so that you no longer hold on to this energy and so you no longer create a reality that confirms it.

The process of purifying your words, thoughts and actions comes with honoring every one of these in a space and in a way that is appropriate and highest aligned. When I interact with others, when I am in service and supporting others, the words that come through, the physical expression that comes forth is not an emotional response but rather a Higher Self response. If a lower aspect of me starts to feel emotional, starts to think or behave in a way that it needs to let out anger, frustration or whatever emotion it is feeling, I allow myself to release this energy as its appropriate in that moment. If this aspect needs me to physically move my body and feel the emotion, yell or scream then I only bring this physically release when I am in a space and place that is appropriate and won't affect anyone else. This is when we gain mastery of ourselves, this is when we don't allow our emotions to inter-fear in our interactions with other people, this is where we don't allow our inner child to come forth and react unconsciously in any situation, instead we bring the best version of ourselves, we bring forth our Highest aspect, our pure love, our peace, our power, our purity, our integrity, our respect and our honor above all things in a way that is needed. This can take make shapes and forms of course and each situation will call for a different response, each experience will be unique and in that moment is when we decide and follow our highest guidance always.

The beauty and magic of all of this is that when we practice and embrace this process we start to create a whole new reality that is based on the peace and purity that we hold. We no longer are afraid of our words, thoughts or actions instead we honor them all and the more that we do, the more we release the emotional energy that might be tied to them; this allows our LightBodies to restore, rebalance and recalibrate our whole entire body, mind and being in a way that allows us to shift our words, thoughts and actions to those that fully support New Earth. It becomes easier and easier and it doesn't even require much thought and has nothing to do with the old sense of control; it becomes a very natural and organic way of being.

Open up to this process and you'll start to feel a complete shift in your entire being that fully supports your Light, your body, your being and especially your New Earth reality.

UNIFY

The perception of separation runs deep in the human body, the individualization of each form creates an illusory perception that each is separated from the whole, separated from all things and yet no matter how physically real sometimes this belief seems it is but only a distorted view of how things truly are. The linear mind is a construct of the ego, it is where separation is perceived, it is the limited aspect of our being that is close minded and close hearted. And yet this is part of the human experience/experiment that we all come down here to break free from... we all come here to liberate ourselves and unify back with all in every way possible.

Each of us are an aspect of Source Creator but the state of consciousness in which one operates from in the 3rd dimensional realm is so limited and narrow minded that we cannot possible conceive this in any way. We each start to remember the more we allow ourselves to move past and expand beyond the current perceptions of the 3D world. This is one of the most challenging things to do as our entire reality is based on the systems and beliefs of this limited world and breaking free means going against everything we thought was true. At the beginning it is scary, we are resistant to it because our 3D world was a world that we thought kept us safe, secure, protected and was transparent but as we start to open up to new and different perspectives we realize that this was far from true. We start to feel how the chaos, the battle, the injustice and the separation of the old world kept us in battle, separation and judgment with each other and even ourselves. The world we thought was safe and secure was only an illusion of the mind that kept us believing in our own limitations, weakness, unworthiness and separation. Yes, the same separation that we perceive in our physical reality is only a reflection of the same separation we have inside.

From the moment we incarnate into a carbon-based body we experience a tangible sensation of separation, we leave the safety of our mother's womb, we drop down in frequency, we detach from Source and we feel the perceived space that lies between all tangible things. One might say that separation feels so very real that our minds completely and totally buy it and hence this becomes one of the core beliefs of our entire existence.

As we continue our human existence the perception of separation continues to grow and expand until the body is no longer able to sustain this concept because deep down it knows that it isn't true. The emotions that we suppress add to the separation, the harsh experiences, the cruel and unjust circumstance that we sometimes find ourselves continue to add to this belief. Regardless of it all we are starting to break free from this illusion. More and more people are starting to feel how the feeling of separation, loneliness, abandonment, seclusion start to feel so incredible off and out of tune deep inside. We start to realize that at the very core of our existence we yearn for connection, we long for unity, we desire the feeling of being close to one another in ways that are pure and loving. Are you starting to feel me on this?

The events that have transpired all around the world have created a much stronger experience that awakens people to the truth of just how connected everything is and how much stronger we are united instead of separated and isolated. The world is finally waking up and so are our own physical bodies. Our internal separation has to dissolve at deep cellular level for then and only then are we going to see the physical unification of the entire human race.

Unifying Inside

The emotional baggage that we suppressed inside of ourselves is in great part the frequency that creates the separation inside. Any emotion that is less that purity, love, peace, joy is a mismatch to our Light, it creates a chemical imbalance, a disharmony, an out of tune melody inside of the body that impedes a natural and organic flow in the body. As one start to awaken, we start to become more sensitive, we start to feel more, we start to sense more and that is because we have numbed every emotion known to man so deep in our bodies that as we start to activate more Light everything gets triggered. You will start to even feel emotions that you didn't even know you had, emotions you thought you had already released, experiences that you thought you had already resolved and although that might be true from one aspect, there are layers to everything so one must be open to diving deeper and deeper into the depths of our being.

The more you open up to every emotion and start to fully feel it with your entire being the more you will start to clear the heaviness and dissolve the separation held at a cellular level. Yes, this goes very deep, down to your DNA. Everything that is not Light has to be completely purged from the body and as it does the barriers, the walls, the doors, the constructs of separation begin to dissolve at deeper and deeper levels from every part of your being. This allows more space inside, this allows for every cell in your body to start to connect and communicate with one another, this allows a deeper connection with every organ, every muscle, every pathway and every fiber of your being. The channels, the flow, the connection of every part of your body start to expand and grow in ways that allows every part of your body to become whole, become integrated and become ONE. It's like that cohesive network of Light finally becomes activated and functional in ways that it never has before. This is how the physical body becomes a miracle machine, completely unified with the field of consciousness that operates above and beyond the linear mind; it becomes capable of anything and everything and has no perceived limitations. It might seem impossible to conceive all of this at this moment but this is part of the evolution that is happening right now in the entire planet.

We are finally becoming unified and as we do we will operate from Unity Consciousness instead of separation consciousness.

MERGE

There is a merging that happens in many levels throughout this journey; a merging of all of your Soul aspects that were broken off, separated, casted away and fragmented. This typically happens throughout our entire human existence and many times without our conscious awareness. The traumas and separated realities that one chooses and experiences in every existence creates a wound, a crack, a fragment that leads to what I call an aspect of yourself "running-away-from-home." It's literally like a teenager or a child that experiences a deep painful experience at home and therefore decides to leave the home because it no longer perceives it to be safe. We all have many of these aspects, this is part of the separation, the misaligned realities and the very thing that creates much pain and suffering in our world. It is our own merging and unification with our own Soul and every one of our Soul aspects that bring forth much Unity inside.

Breaking Free

There are many constructs and belief systems within that created a reality with many rules and laws and these created a mold, an identity of how one should be, how one should behave, what one should do, what is acceptable and unacceptable, and much more. Every time we fall short of these rules we begin to deny ourselves, deny how we feel, hide our emotions and separate off because we believe that that version of ourselves is not worthy, unacceptable and not deserving of love and support.

This is where breaking free from every old construct, instilled belief system, passed down value must be completely eradicated from ones life. This is where the breaking away of the old perceptions and breaking away of the old rules and limitations is necessary in order to allow ourselves to honor each version of who we are, what we've been, what we've done and what we've allowed. The old earth realities were based on duality constructs that lend to a mentality in which good and bad, right and wrong are the foundational pillars that create a peaceful and balance society when in reality this constructs and systems only amplified the belief that we had to separate and condemn the versions of ourselves that didn't live up to the expectations of societal norms. All of these systems have the embedded belief that "I am not good enough", "I am not worthy or valuable enough" which creates a deep emotional turmoil that one tries to run away from. Yes, the running away from our emotions, is parallel to our Soul aspects running away from home, we've been running away from ourselves for far too long. We've been hiding ourselves away because we have not come to fully love, accept and honor every single part of ourselves and it is only when we break free from the old perceptions of old earth systems that we start to fully inner-stand and remember that our actions and behaviors don't make us who we are, they don't dictate our worth or are value and nothing truly can.

The way we have acted or behaved in the perceived past has a much deeper root and when we are able to see our intentions behind each act, each word and each reaction we will start to see that deep down inside is just a version of ourselves that is traumatized, that is carrying an enormous amount of hurt, anger, pain, suffering that has not been resolved. Every single time we let an emotion sit inside of us without fully honoring it and feeling it all the way through it sits and rots inside of us creating a force of resistance, this force becomes so loud and so heavy that it blinds us, it blocks us from seeing others and it pushes us to live our lives from the emotional turmoil still held inside. In reality this force is a version of ourselves that is screaming and yelling for attention and it utilizes emotional triggers so that we start to feel and connect with the very same aspect that one is trying to run away from and/or suppress.

The more we start to honor our emotions and feel them fully the more we start to break free from the chains and cords of an enslaved reality that keeps triggering them. Now more than ever all of the old systems are breaking down and dismantling before our very eyes and in that we get to break those same systems inside of our own bodies and minds.

We are finally starting to feel our emotions, connect with the aspects of ourselves that have run away and merge them back inside.

Our Bodies

The tightness and rigidity of our own physical bodies equates to the structures that were held in place by the old ways. In essence think of it like living in a house full of rules and laws that told you exactly what to say, when to breathe, when to sleep, what to do, what to wear, what to eat, when to go outside, literally a prison cell where one's one desires, needs and wants were not honored at all but suppressed. When one lives in a place with so many rules one starts to feel unloved, unsupported, unvalued and unworthy and therefore decides to leave home.

As we each open up to each phase of the process we start to remember that our bodies are what held the linear and limited constructs that we all ran way at some level. This is where we start to realize that focusing on our physical bodies, the tightness of our muscles, the pains and aches and start to fully connect with every part of ourselves is extremely important in every way. The more the body becomes free inside from all the old structures the more flow, the more freedom, the more balance, the more flexibility, the more love and respect we get to experience in every level. We start to create a home within that is based on the purity, the love, the joy, the peace that we truly are. As your physical body becomes less and less entangled with the old ways and starts to embrace the new ones, the new Light frequencies, the new structures that give full and total freedom to every aspect of ourselves, our Soul aspects start to come back home. They start to feel the support, sense the love, open up to the peace and merge back to all that they are.

The physical body and the physical environment that surrounds you go hand in hand. As the physical body starts to relax more, open up more, surrender more, trust more everything in your environment starts to shift and change and recode to reflect that back. We start to hold more respect for all that surrounds us and we start to treat it differently, we start to let go of things/objects that no longer bring peace, we start to free ourselves from the old and we start to bring/call forth all that does. We start to spend more time in nature, with people that fully support us, we start to change our jobs, occupations and/or work environment, we start to shift our entire reality because we start to feel how the old one is no longer acceptable, it no longer brings us the joy and peace that our Soul and heart's desire. This starts to create a whole new experience, with blessings, synchronicities, magical encounters and exciting new opportunities that we create because of all the re-alignments that we choose to do in our own physical bodies as well as our physical environments.

The more you focus inward, the more you'll start to choose in a way that fully supports your Light and everything in your reality will start to shift so that it truly supports you, your LightBody, New Earth and all that you are.

BE

The being state is a normal and natural part of who we are. It is the part of us that knows and remembers, it is the essence in us that is fully connected in every moment to all that is. It is in holding this frequency that all starts to shift and re-align in a way that is so beautiful and magical.

There is an important phase of this process in which everything that kept you busy and distracted from BEing starts to fall away, dissipate and no longer exist. In essence everything that was part of the old 3D reality was meant to keep you so disconnected from yourself that it created this push and pull force in which made us believe that we had to be always doing something if not we were lazy, unproductive and unworthy of everything. When the old structures start to collapse inside and more Light activates within, you will start to feel a peace that you've never felt before, a stillness, a quietness and in that space you start to honor it like never before. You start to want more of that in your reality; the old ways of believing that we needed to be always busy and occupied amongst the hustle and bustle of cities and noise starts to dissolve. You begin to recognize what amplifies the inner peace inside and what doesn't and all of a sudden your priorities change.

In the old 3D reality, being busy and always doing stuff kept us distracted, fearful and preoccupied in building a reality that we believed was going to make us happier when it was quite the opposite. It kept us from going deeper within ourselves, feeling our emotions and having a deep sense of connection with what our bodies, our Soul's and our hearts truly wanted. The more disconnected we are from ourselves the more connected we are to a world that told us what we needed to be, do and have in order to be successful and accomplished. As you start to disconnect from the old world the more you start to establish a connection within yourself and that opens up a whole new feeling, remembrance and value.

5D= Being State

As we continue to hold more Light inside of our physical bodies and field we start to anchor more of the frequencies of pure peace and pure Love. These frequencies equate to the 5D/Christ Consciousness frequencies where you breathe and dance and merge with the essence of the present moment. There is a stillness inside that brings everything to a halt and awakens within you this magical flow that exists in each moment. You start to move, eat, talk, see, feel in a whole different way. Each moment becomes a gift and with it there is nothing more to focus on, nothing more to do, nothing more to accomplish. It is in observing and becoming fully aware of each moment through the sacred BEingness that each moment unfolds, opens up and becomes a pure flow of peace, magic and love. This isn't to say that other emotions won't come up because they will but it is in being fully present and aware and honoring of each and every emotion that they start to dissolve and dissipate. Becoming fully present allows you to be more conscious of when an emotion comes up and as it does you honor it by being with it, feeling it fully and allowing the entire body to do what it needs to release it and clear it so that it no longer stays suppressed inside of the body.

Being present isn't about only focusing on the "good" or denying when things feel off, it is in being fully present that you can actually recognize the lightness or heaviness of each frequency that presents itself and as you open up you'll start to receive the guidance you need that will assist you in knowing what to do next to shift things back into alignment.

Continue to open up to these magical frequencies that are who you are at your core and as you do everything will shift back to support you in every way.

A New Foundation

This Being state is the new foundation of our New Earth reality, it is the basis of everything. As you start to hold more and more of it inside your whole body/being it becomes a part of who you are and how you function on New Earth. The old foundations become obsolete, they become no more and we no longer hold them in our body. This is how we also start to shift our "exterior" reality and although there are still many people that function from fear and lack we become the new species that evolve out of that system/mentality into a brand new one.

The new way of being becomes one that is rooted in pure love and sacred connection with all beings and all things. We no longer feed off of each other, diminish, suppress and oppress our Light but rather the opposite; we support one another, embrace, uplift, assist and unite as One.

The new foundation must be continuously anchored in, this takes full focus, energy and commitment as it goes against what the old ways taught us. It isn't an overnight thing and it takes everything we have for the mind/ego will continue to fight back and revert back to the old ways because it perceives them as comfortable and safe. The ego used to feed off of the old structure of fear, lack, judgement, victimhood and so much more but as one starts to break from the old, these mentalities start to dissolve and so does our ego for it merges back inside of our Soul/heart. Our Soul/Higher self now starts to lead the way, build a whole new foundation in which one can be of full support and service to others in their own special and unique way.

There is much to accomplish and share but it's important to remember that one's own journey back to a BEing state is crucial as that allows us to be in our own pure essence in every moment.

As one continues to anchor these frequencies and become fully emerged and present in the now, the ideas, inspirations, support, guidance and much more will start to flow through. It is in the full allowance of the BEing state that one starts to re-align with the actions, projects, service works that will support one's own Light/LightBody and the whole entire planet as well. The stillness, the quietness, the calmness and peace that one experiences as one becomes fully present opens up each quantum's field of infinite possibilities and endless opportunities. It is then and only then that we each start to open up and focus our energy in that which supports and amplifies our Light and other's Light as well. So keep opening up and allowing these massive flow of 5D frequencies that are pouring through right now so that we can continue to anchor them into the physical body.

DO

The Doing state comes after the Being state. The BEing is the state in which we are fully opened and allowing of everything that is occurring and in that openness we receive, we receive the guidance, the inner knowing, the inner wisdom, the remembrance, the codes and messages needed in order to move forward. After these are received we begin a process of shifting, moving, re-aligning, clearing everything in our reality that supports that which we saw so that we can materialize it.

The doing state comes in many stages and phases of our entire journey. When we were asleep and unconscious our doing state was fueled from the lack and fear that we held inside, we made choices based on what our family/parents/society told us was good, safe and expected, we created a reality that was based on material gains, identities, titles, societal roles and more that only created more fear and lack. We didn't truly know how to listen to our hearts and therefore we ended up listening to everything and everyone outside of ourselves that told us what to be, do and have. As we become more conscious of who we are and why we are here we start to realize that everything that we focused on, worked hard for and wanted didn't truly make us happy. A lot of the things that we focused on weren't even something we wanted to do in the first place and we only did those things because we were told we needed to in order to be successful and have financial security.

As we being to awaken, become more aware of what truly makes us happy we start to open up to the possibility that following our heart isn't something to be scared of, it isn't something to deny or suppress but rather something we must honor. This allows us to live from a place of peace and wholeness that the old realities didn't fulfill.

Shifting Out of Unconsciousness

This entire journey is about shifting to a state of full consciousness in every way. When we lived in our 3D realities we were fully unconscious unaware of ourselves, unaware of our choices and intent, unaware of what was true in our heart and so we lived blindly and carelessly wanting the recognition of a world that didn't even honor our Soul. It is through our awakening that we start to become a little more conscious, we start to feel more, remember more and choose things differently. Yes, there is still many unconscious aspects that are running in the forefront of our realities but we start to become more aware of our surroundings, our relationships, our occupations, our desires and which ones support our peace and joy and which ones create more stress and worry in our life. This is when we start taking action, we start to re-align things in our reality, let go of things, relationships, jobs, we start to feel everything we had suppressed inside and we start to dissolve the energy that created much resistance and held us back from actually listening and honoring our Soul.

As one starts to navigate the 4D realm there is much that one has to physically, emotionally and energetically move so that our entire realities start to shift, dissolve and reconstruct with those that are new, Soul-aligned, peaceful and pure.

REALIGN

The re-alignment of one's entire reality is necessary in every level. It is a constant thing as one starts to see/feel/sense more of what was out of alignment, what was in the way of one's peace, what was creating havoc and stress in ones world and as you start to recognize this you start to make the necessary choices and changes so that your whole life is fully aligned at a Soul level.

Inner to Outer Re-Alignment

This inner and outer re-alignment happens simultaneously throughout this journey. Once you start to awaken and consciously ascend you will start to feel your way through your reality and start to see and recognize what is amplifying your life/Light and what is sucking/depleting it. It is important to remember that your ego/linear mind will be challenged in every way, your fears and worries will surface and you will be faced with everything that will show you more of what is blocking you from fully re-aligning your life. This takes lots of focus, commitment and patience as there are many things to feel and resolve inside but remember that everything is fully supporting you and the more you allow yourself to go deeper within the stronger you will come out on the other side.

The carbon-based, human body stores an enormous amount of emotions, illusions, programs that are part of the separation held inside. This separation brings about much imbalance and aligned our entire reality to that of the 3D world. All the fear and lack inside created a physical experience that made that illusion more real and it spins us into loop cycles and karmic bonds that keep us bound to lower states of consciousness.

As you continue to feel and sense more the dissolution and clearing of the ties, cords, contracts and old programs becomes less and less heavy. As these blocks dissolve the body has more space to move, to flow, to balance itself and allow a harmonious flow of energy and influx of Light to pour through. Every cell, every atom, every molecule, every fiber, bone and muscle must be re-aligned with our Soul/Higher Heart/Higher Mind so that each is intrinsically connected to the flow of your pure Light and as this occurs the old 3D gridding system starts to fall apart, collapse and level at a deep cellular level.

The exterior re-alignment of one's physical reality becomes much easier when your inner world continually breaks down the separation in your body. It is a process and takes much practice but as one progresses the guidance that comes through from inside will be much easier to hear and the actualization of each guidance step will be much easier to execute. You won't have the heaviness of the beliefs and programs that used to tie us down, block us and hold us back instead you will have the inner knowing and courage to start taking those bold action steps that you know will support you in creating a much more peaceful, joyous, loving experience that will fully support your LightBody and ascension process. You will no longer care about what others say or think, you won't be pulled by what society says you should do, you will deal with your ego/linear mindset as it comes up and you will open up your heart more and more so that you can receive all the support and guidance you need.

Both your inner and outer reality will constantly shift and re-align as you continually open up and allow it and as you do everything will change. You will start to feel it inside and you will start to see it all around you in every way. Your entire world will never be the same because your state of consciousness will drastically shift your perception of everything and it will allow you to have a more sacred awareness of all that is unfolding in your life and in the entire world.

This is a process that each person has to do. Nobody can do it for you because we each have to return back to our own Mastery and full state of consciousness so that we can remember that we are Creator Beings and that we have the power to shift anything back to purity. We let go of the savior and victimhood programs and we start to take full charge of who we are and our entire reality. Every person has the responsibility to create in a way that is Highest Aligned and one that creates peace in every level. The more we start to remember this and the more conscious actions we take towards our inner journey the faster this will occur.

REMEMBER

Coming down into this very dense and physical human body created much separation inside that we forgot everything. We forgot who we are, where we come from, what our purposes are, and so much more. As we start to awaken, we start to resonate with people and truths that hit a cord inside. We may not fully comprehend it, we may not fully believe it at first, we might think we are crazy and losing it and it is all a normal part of the process. The essence of who we are and what we are capable is so beyond that of our human intellect can comprehend and way more than what we have been taught by normal standards in our 3D society. In many ways we all have to break out of the old, break away from the system and break our minds free from the old constructs. It takes a lot to do this and it is a process.

We are all being gifted opportunities in which to see more in our own reality that don't align with who we are anymore. Our jobs, relationships, identities just don't seem to fit anymore, they don't bring us lasting peace and true fulfillment and this is us how we start to remember that there is more… there is more to this, there is more to our existence, there is more to this world and pretty much everything.

Opening up our hearts and minds will allow us to start to remember. It may come at first as just a feeling inside that makes us feel at home and then it grows more and more and more and we start to see/hear more things that start to ring a bell.

Everything is held deep inside of our bodies but with all the density we hold it got buried deep inside without us being aware of it and without us being able to access it. The more you start to feel everything heavy, everything tight, everything discordant inside of your body you will begin to release, dissolve and peel off the layers and layers of density that separated you from your Light. Light is who you are, it is a frequency that holds much information, much knowledge and much wisdom. As we start to access more of our deep inner Light we will start to remember more and more and more.

All the knowledge of the entire Universe is literally held inside, it is in our DNA. The amount of information that can be stored in a single DNA strand is so vast and much greater than what our liner minds can hold. This is one of the reasons why our DNA has been so suppressed but now more than ever we are unlocking it, activating and accessing more of it.

Sacred Remembrance

There is a phase of the process where you get to access all the knowledge from inside rather than "out there." All of the Light that comes through your body allows an activation that opens up the cells and as this occurs your body is able to process and decipher all the Lightcodes and all the information that is already stored within your body. At the beginning we believe we get the information from "outside" of ourselves because we don't fully comprehend that we have this information inside, but as we start to open up more and more we start to retrieve and share information from inside as part of our deep sacred remembrance.

It's all a process, first we awaken and we start to research and dive deep into the world of spirituality however we are guided and called. This is a very important part of the process as it feels like we have found something that we've been looking for all along our existence. We become hungry for more, we start to read and watch and listen to tons and tons of content and all of this is important as it activates us inside. As one continues we must start to regain trust in ourselves again, trust in our inner messages and guidance and as you do you start to detract from searching "out there" so much and rather you start to focus more inward. The more you connect from deeper within the more access you will have to the information that you already hold. We come to finally remove all of the road blocks, barriers and walls so we can finally access the doors to our own golden Library of ancient knowledge.

As we continue to access more information there are remembrances that will come up that will trigger a lot in us and that's a normal part of the process. Anything that we still hold inside especially memories and experiences that are still unbalanced, unresolved or distorted must be fully felt and cleared. It is important to not let the ego in and make us believe that what we are remembering isn't true because this will continue to suppress it. It doesn't matter what it is that you remember what matters is that you open up to feel every single emotion that is still attached to it. The emotion is what creates the separation and keeps this loop cycle alive so give yourself permission to feel it all. These will break you free from the bonds and open you up to a much more Soul aligned reality in every way.

As more of our sacred remembrances come forth and we dissolve everything that keeps us bonded to the old we start to recognize that everything that we chose had a much higher reason and purpose and we start to hold a deeper peace and love towards ourselves and everyone involved as well. The essence of who we truly are cannot ever be broken or marred and so the more we continue to reconnect more and more with all that we are the more we return to live and exist as so.

BRIDGE

Because there is so much separation held inside we must reconnect everything back and as we do we become the bridge that unites all. We are the BridgeKeepers of New Earth; we become the Bridge that reconnects every aspect, every organ, every cell back to the purity of your Higher Heart. The bridge to New Earth is inside and it is up to each and every person to activate it themselves by going deeper within and breaking all the barriers, systems and programs.

The illusory 3D reality that we created was all based on separation; everything was disconnected and therefore unconscious. As we begin to open up we start to feel more, we sense more and as we do we start to release more, let go of more and dissolve the barriers and the walls inside that separated us.

The Rainbow Bridge

Rainbows are extremely powerful to work with. It doesn't matter if they are up in the sky, or coming from the sun, or being reflected from a window, these frequencies activate one's own Rainbow inside or Rainbow LightBody. It activates each energy center or chakra at a deeper level so that it continues to open up more and more. Each energy center must be fully cleared, re-aligned and expanded so that they can reconnect back to your higher heart and merge into a beautiful pillar of Light.

When all your energy centers completely open up and merge they become the Rainbow Bridge which then opens up a huge portal for you to walk through and cross over to the other side. The more we hold this Rainbow Bridge inside the more we are able to cross every part and aspect of ourselves over to New Earth/5D/Heaven. We must fully become the Rainbow Bridge inside and as we do more magic starts to unfold.

When you hold these frequencies deeper and deeper within and they become who you are you'll be able to experience and create a physical Rainbow in the sky that reflects back the Rainbow that you have become. I had one of the most powerful experiences with this where I activated all of the Rainbow frequencies inside, opened up my heart portal and was able to create my very own physical Rainbow Bridge in the sky. After so much rain and drizzles and me holding on to the Rainbow frequencies within, a huge hail storm came through and after that the sun peaked through and created three magical full Rainbows in the sky. This was super powerful and it was through this Rainbow Bridge and Portal that I was able to walk through and cross over aka ascension of consciousness (physical ascension is the next phase of the process).

We all have this capability but we forgot. Now it is time to remember and become the Rainbow Bridge ourselves so that we can completely leave the old one behind and live and experience New Earth fully.

RELEASE

    In our old realities, we believed that we needed to hold on, keep tight, not let go of everything in some level. We created a reality in which we valued keeping and holding on to things, emotions, memories, people even when deep down inside we knew that they were creating stress in our world. We all have this unconscious and subconscious fear deep inside that keeps us from truly letting go and releasing ourselves from all the pain and hurt. We hold on unconsciously because somewhere deep inside we believe that that keeps us safe, it keeps us hidden, it keeps us from being seen, it keeps us from utilizing our pure power and actually taking responsibility for our reality.

    Releasing is a huge part of this entire process that we come to embrace; every moment presents you with an opportunity to see and feel what is in alignment and what isn't in alignment with your Soul/Light. We constantly have to release ourselves from things, feelings, energies that keep us bound and anchored to the old. The reality is that when you start to open up to release you actually release yourself from the bonds and chains that are keeping you locked up and enslaved. It isn't anyone else's responsibility to free us but our own. We must give ourselves permission to do this as sometimes we have aspects of ourselves that are waiting, waiting for mom and dad to love us fully for who we are, waiting for our old partners to say sorry, waiting for people to change and this only keeps us from moving the energy ourselves and becoming free. We must set ourselves free in every way instead of holding on to an energy that only creates more pain and suffering for us and not anyone else.

The Releasing Process

The process of releasing takes many forms and can be done in countless ways. There is no right or wrong way to do it, you essentially open up to every method and do it. Sometimes some work better than others, at times we have to find new ones because as we evolve so does our practices. In time, we create our own tools and practices and share them too.

Remember that with everything there is a physical, emotional, mental and energetic level that one must work with (at least before ascending because afterwards these all merge and become One body). We must open each body for a full clearing. There is a lot of physical purging that we must go through that deeply and greatly supports this process. Anything material that keeps you tied to an emotion, a belief or memory must be released from your reality so that you are no longer tied to it. This may bring up an emotional release which is a very necessary part of the process as well, all the emotions that we had deeply suppressed to those things, to the people or the memories of those objects finally start to pour out of us and we must honor them all by fully feeling them with our entire body/being. The mental release can happen through the emotional release but I've recognized within myself that another process that has supported me enormously is writing, writing all my thoughts, the words, the expressions, the beliefs that many aspects still hold inside has been a great way to mentally release these energies from my mental body. After I write it all out, I do a burning bowl ceremony and burn all the pages for a deeper closure and release.

Again   it doesn't matter what or how your process is what matters is that you continuously open up more to new ones, new ways, new methods, and keep feeling everything so that your LightBody can continue to activate and support the deeper levels of cellular release and physical body clearing.

Cellular Release

This particular release is one that is simultaneously happening all the time as you continue to release at an emotional, mental, physical and energetic level. The Light codes that start to come through into your body will assist in the cellular release that is needed.

Our conscious minds are nowhere near as advanced and knowledgeable of what this process entails and so therefore we must constantly surrender, allow and let go of anywhere we are still wanting to control this process. Your Light knows exactly what to do and it just needs us to not inter-fear with the process which is why a lot of the time it will knock you down so you rest and sleep. Sleeping greatly supports this process as your conscious mind is not able to think. You want to continue to let go of thinking in every way possible so that your ego/linear mind doesn't sink into the fears and worries.

This process is not linear and it isn't "normal" or comfortable through the eyes of our ego and so it fears it to the point that it can lock itself, tightens the muscles and therefore slows down the process. This is where we each have to truly challenge ourselves to fully surrender and let go of our need to know, and control everything. If we continue to do this we will only prolong the pain and keep us bound to mentality that keeps us believing we are suffering or something "bad" is happening to us.

Open up to every phase of this process and as you do you will start to have a much better and deeper inner standing of all that is going on. The more conscious you are and the more willing you are to fully allow this process the more enjoyable and the more exciting this will become.

RECONNECT

There is a deep reconnection that occurs in many many levels and in many ways. The reason we have disconnected ourselves from nature and from others is because we have a deep level of separation going on inside. Our DNA has been shut down and suppressed in a way that the information needed in order for our bodies to function at an optimal level while holding the entirety of our Soul/Light has been lacking. We have 12 DNA strands but only 2 are active, the rest is what is sometimes referred to as "junk DNA" but it is far from it. Think of your DNA as a book shelve, with only two book shelves active there isn't much space for many books, aka information, to be stored as opposed to the number of books that can be stored with 12 shelves. These 10 shelves have been laying dormant for a long time and they are finally starting to become active, they are waking up and bringing forth much more information that is needed for your entire body/field to be recoded in such a way that supports your Light.

Cellular Reconnection

As more of our dormant DNA comes online there is a restructuring that must occur at a deep cellular level. It may not seem apparent because we can't physically see our cells without a microscope but inside all of our cells and organs haven't been able to communicate with one another. They each have stored layers and layers of deeply suppressed emotions, unconscious thoughts and programs and all of this created walls and barriers that block our cells from being able to communicate with one another.

The more Light that comes through into our bodies the more our DNA is restored in a way that is able to transmit codes of information to all the cells in our body. This information awakens the cells, the organs, the muscles in ways that allows us to feel more. Now more than ever there is a massive amount of people that are starting to feel deeper, they are becoming more sensitive but that is a very important and necessary part of this entire process because everything was so asleep that we closed ourselves from feeling all the heaviness inside. The more we open up to feeling it all the more we become aware of what is going on inside; the more these suppressed and unresolved emotions get triggered the more we get consciously engage in the releasing process.

Re-Connecting with All

As we start to reconnect at a deeper level inside we are going to start to remember how to reconnect with everything and every part of our selves. We start to treat things and others differently because we start to recognize the connection we have with them. Yes, we each have a physical body that seem to be separate from all other things but in reality everything has the same energy, the same essence and we all become a reflection of one another.

The essence of pure love is within all, no exceptions; however the perception that we may have towards a particular thing or experience either unites us or separates us. Anything that we believe to be bigger, more powerful or even scary we tend to run away from, we turn our backs, we hide from it or we pretend its not there. This separates us from being able to remember why it is there, what it is trying to show us and how it is supporting us. If you would let go of all judgments towards anything and everything that you have and just be with it, connect in a space where you feel fully loved and supported much magic will come from it. No matter what it is, when you open yourself to fully connecting with it, whether it's an emotion, an experience, an object, anything at all, there is a powerful reaction that occurs deeper than our minds can comprehend that awakens and activates at a Soul level. We start to receive information and sacred remembrances as to what it represents, what it holds, what it is trying to show us, what it serves, who is it supporting and much much more. If we start to open up and listen, feel, see there is a slew of information that will come forth that will allow you and support you so that you can break free from any old bonds and illusions.

Our mind keeps us stuck in the fear and the lack and it makes us believe that connecting is a scary and dangerous thing. We have to move into a space where we can open ourselves more and more and remember that we are everything therefore nothing is and ever will be bigger than us; it is only our old perceptions that keep us from remembering this. There is nothing to protect from anymore because we start to realize how powerful we are and that everything "out there" that seems threatening is only an aspect of you trying to show you something that you still have yet to see or remember.

Keep opening up, keep surrendering deeper inside so that you can continue to re-connect with everything and as you do you will start to have a much more meaningful and fulfilling human experience.

RESOLVE

We must resolve everything that is at some level heavy, less than pure love and painful. We programmed this 3D reality in ways that made us believe that we weren't good enough and somehow if we held on to the painful and traumatic experiences in life we would be safe and good enough to be loved and supported. It is quite backwards for sure. The holding on to it, the suppressing it, the not wanting to feel it only re-creates it in our reality until we consciously choose to resolve it inside and fully dissolve all the cords and emotional attachments.

Victim and Narcissistic Mentalities

These are both very similar frequencies but expressed from completely opposite ends of the spectrum. We don't recognize them as such though but it is time that we do. These forms of control and manipulation are deeply instilled in all of us whether we recognize it, believe it, admit it or not. These frequencies are ancient energies that we all came here to release and dissolve so we don't recreate the same old loop cycles and realities that keep us small and powerless.

It is important to tap into these frequencies deeper inside of the body so that we can start to resolve all of the "past" experiences, memories, stories and emotions that still keep us tied to them. Remember that the ego aspects love to be small, love the drama and trauma, love control and manipulation because it lives in a world where it believes that there is no other way, no other choice but to keep being small and fragile. As you continue to feel everything at a deeper level and you start to connect with these aspects you will start to see/feel that the ones holding on to these frequencies are just our inner child aspects that are so scared, so terrified, so angry, so sad that their darkness shows up and runs the show. This is about reconnecting back with these aspects that all they every wanted growing up is a little attention from their parents, or they wanted to be loved and accepted for who they are and this is where we each get to gift that to them. We become our own Divine Mom and Dad figure, the one we never had when we were growing up; this is part of each person's responsibility.

We don't sit around and wait for others to love us, we don't sit and blame others or repeat our own tragic stories over and over for attention, no, we reconnect with these aspects as the Higher versions of ourselves and we pour all of our love into them in the way that they most need. These aspects don't remember who they are, they don't remember that they are worthy and enough and it is up to each and every single one of us to remind them, to show them, to gift them what they need in order for them to start opening up and start dissolving all the stories they are carrying inside.

Every single one of us chose their own harsh and traumatic experience at a Soul level because it is just part of how we get to fully clear it from all of our existences. In order to bring the entire planet and collective back to a state of pure peace and love we have to clear every single one of our unresolved existences, distorted timelines, suppressed emotions and so much more.

As we continue to evolve this may change so don't affix to anything but for now this is the way it works. The more you open up to these aspects the faster you will start to resolve everything inside from every level, every dimension, every reality and every existence that you have every lived whether you remember it or not. This is about balancing everything we have every created back to a state of purity and it takes resolving all of our experiences so that we can recreate all brand new ones that support our Light and serves the entire planet.

There is much to resolve inside in many levels but it takes just one conscious choice of opening up to it and the more that you do the faster all occurs.

ANCHOR

The density of your physical body created a gravitational pull that kept you anchored to the 3rd dimensional state of consciousness. Everything from heavy emotions, old beliefs and programs, fear and lack based structures are frequencies that anchor you down into the lower realms. As you start to dissolve all of the heaviness and separation we start to detach from everything of the old and we start to anchor the frequencies of our pure Soul/Light that simultaneously anchor us into the higher realms, higher dimensional states of consciousness.

Your level of consciousness dictates what realm you exist and which one you are anchored in. Your words, your thoughts, your actions, your emotions are all clues that will assist you in recognizing where you are functioning from and that will dictate your physical reality experience. The more you observe yourself in every way the more you are able to shift and change things in a way that is most appropriate without forcing or controlling the process. When an emotion or thought comes up that is less than loving we tend to push it away, hide it, suppress it or disown it. This creates much heaviness and resistance that keeps you bound to a reality that keeps recreating similar experiences or loop cycles. When you open yourself to just allow all to come through, emotions, thoughts, words, they are only coming forth to show you an energy that you still hold inside. Sometimes we like to think that they aren't ours or they didn't come from us and that may keep us from fully owning it. If an energy comes forth as a thought or an emotion then something within got activated which means somewhere inside you have that same energy. Most of these energies are ancient which means they got passed on from other existences that are still actively playing that distortion out and it is in this current existence that we get to fully clear it so that we are no longer playing out karmic distortions.

The more we see, recognize and fully own this energy as something that is somewhere inside of us the more we have the ability to shift and dissolve it to where it no longer plays a role in our reality. This is where we each have to take our power back and not play small, or become the victims anymore. We have to take full responsibility for everything that comes into our field because it is only an aspect of an energy that we haven't fully honored or remembered its purpose in our reality.

Anchoring into the New

The Light frequencies that are coming through into our planet right now are highly assisting us in anchoring us back into New Earth. This Light is our Soul, it is activating our purity and returning us to living as Souls again. As we continue to open up to our Soul and Light the more we are able to let go and completely detach from the old structures from every level of our being.

Every time we anchor more and more Light into our vessel we will receive more information and more awareness as to what we need to physically shift and re-align in our reality. Everything from relationships, jobs, identities, material objects that kept us tied to an old version of ourselves must be fully released from our reality so that we can fully dissolve all of the belief systems and identities that made us believe we needed those things to survive, be loved or accepted.

The more Light we allow inside of our bodies the more the old structures dissolve and the more we are able to anchor these New Earth frequencies inside. New Earth is an energy that fully matches our Soul, it is aligned with Christ Consciousness and Higher state of consciousness that support all that is pure, peaceful and loving. As we open ourselves up and increase our vibrational frequency through the anchoring of our Light we start to experience the magic, the beauty, the peace, the harmony and joy of a New Earth reality.

RELAX

Relaxing throughout this entire process is another huge activator that goes deep into your cells and allows an opening to occur in which to release and allow more Light to pour through your body. Because our physical body already came with a lot of density and heaviness in order to incarnate it must go through a continual process of relaxation so that every organ, every muscle, every cell can purge and detox the enormous amount of toxins and discord held inside. Every word, every thought, every emotion, every belief and system that links up to the 3D realms needs to be dissolved fully from every part of the body so one can have enough room for our Soul/Light to come through.

At first it can be as simple as just resting, sleeping, being outdoors or doing something you enjoy. All of these things will assist in relaxing your body. Becoming conscious of when your body tenses up is highly important too because then you start to become more observant as to what triggered this response. Everything in your reality that was linked up to the old gridding systems connects to your body and causes more tension, more fear, lack and stress. As we start to recognize the things, people, environment, hobbies that create this kind of response the more we have to consciously remove and realign everything in a way that is highest aligned so that we can no longer expose ourselves and our bodies to energies that will keep us tied down and in fear.

Muscles

Everything and anything that is fear and lack based locks us up, it paralyzed us and it creates tightness in the body. The tighter your muscles are, the more density/heaviness you are holding on to and the harder it is to move, to change, to see, to feel, to shift your reality. Your muscles hold the gridding system of your reality and so these become a focal point in your journey. Before, in the old days, we used to patronize wanting tight/lean muscles, or a six pack or a muscular figure but as you continue to open up to this process you start to realize that all that tightness created a reality that was just as tight and rigid.

When I went all in on my journey I realized that the body needed an enormous amount of rest and sleep and I had no desire to work out anymore. I didn't question it, I didn't fight or resist it I just went with the flow and as I continued to navigate and learn more along the way I started to connect the dots. I realized just how much by body needed to continuously relax and so I had to let go of any sort of fitness routine. Luckily I had already gone through that phase right before my LightBody activated when I started to be very focused and consistent about working out and that is a normal phase that occurs right before our LightBody activates. I wanted to mention that because if you are in that phase then honor it. There will be other phases where you won't have the energy or desire to work out anymore and this will be just as important because your entire muscular system has to break down and release all the old 3D gridding systems and not engaging in heavy duty muscle work out will greatly assist.

This is another big reversal that also occurs. In the old days we were so focused on "fixing, improving" our physique but not from a pure intention, it was mostly because we didn't think we were good enough or perfect just as we were. We valued looks over our pure essence, we wanted to look a certain way, be a certain size, look like someone else, and so much more. We did not learn to care for our bodies in a way that it fully honors and respects what it actually needs in order to hold our Soul/Light. When you start to fully listen, tune in and honor your body, you'll start to give it what it needs and as you do your body will start to release all that it no longer needs. Everything held in place by your muscular system starts to be released, and therefore your muscles start to relax and your body becomes come in-tuned, connected and activated.

Your Physical World

Focus and observe everything in your physical reality world, whatever creates more fear and lack has to be removed because your body is holding on to the structure of the gridding system that is holding it in place. The more you remove everything that is heavy, dense, fear based the more your muscles are able to relax and unwind.

Nature and all things natural, pure and organic are huge elements that will assist you in relaxing your muscles. The more your body is surrounded by things that are pure and feed the Soul the more your body feels like it can open up and relax. We are each responsible in creating a sacred space in every way possible so that our bodies feel the love and support that we may not have felt as we were growing up. Now it is time to create this on our own so our inner child feels safe. If you can equate your physical body with being your inner/wounded child this will make a huge difference. When you consistently create a space in which your body can feel comforted, can open up and relax your inner child will feel this also and will start to release all the heaviness and trauma that it has been holding on for years.

Remember that the more you body opens up the more your

Light can come through; well this is also very important for your inner child. The more your body opens and anchors more Light the more your inner child can integrate and merge back with your Soul/heart so that you no longer operate from this separated aspect. You then start to operate from your pure and whole essence and as a result you get to create a whole new reality for yourself and share your pure Love with all those around you.

Magical is an understatement to all of the beautiful things that occur when you fully allow your body/muscles to open up and relax and although there are many emotions that will also get activated and triggered, feeling is another huge release that will support you in many ways. Continue to allow, surrender and relax fully throughout this whole process and you'll start to see how things start to shift and change faster than you thought possible.

BALANCE

We must become balanced, retune all energies, purify all distortions and clear all suppressed emotions. Becoming fully balanced means returning to live as Light. Yes, we have both Light and Dark inside but this doesn't mean that we have to have an equal amount of both frequencies to be balanced but quite the contrary. Our Dark is our ego, our separation and when that is actively playing out, coming out and controlling our realities we create a very imbalanced and distorted world. Our Darkness must be dissolved and returned back to its pure form so that our Light shines fully and re-balances everything out.

Balance comes from within, it's what we hold inside and where we operate from. It isn't a balance that follows the old rules and perceptions, it goes far beyond that. As we increase our Light quotient or level the amount of sleep and rest that one must allow may seem very unbalanced and yet this is necessary in order to create more balance inside. The old world won't comprehend this in any way and that's ok. In order to revert all of the old beliefs and concepts we must do the exact opposite of what we were told was "right" in order to fully break free from that mentality and simultaneously create a new template inside that honors and embraces that which the old 3D world did not.

Health Imbalances

For most of our reality we functioned from fear, lack and separation, we kept ourselves hidden and suppressed which created many imbalances inside. These imbalances created much dis-ease in the body and as a result we placed many labels on ourselves. Our bodies are intelligent, they know exactly what to do and how to repair themselves but with the heaviness all around they aren't able to move, maneuver and function in the ways that are needed for the body to be healthy.

As we allow more Light to integrate and fully anchor inside of our bodies we create more balance and everything starts to reconnect and communicate with one another in ways that fully support the LightBody.

Karma

Karma is simply an imbalance of energies. We all have them whether are conscious of it or not; we all have played unconscious realities that created much distortion and suffering. We must now fully balance and re-align everything so that we are no longer playing in the unconscious karmic loops, cycles and debts.

Think of an existence in which you abused our own power, you utilized your own energy against people and nature; these actions created much imbalances. Now you must clear those distortions of energy that are held inside of your body so that you can restore your pure power and utilize it in ways that are supportive, appropriate and for the good of all.

The karmic contracts that we created to play out here are also distorted and so if we played a role where we abused our power then in this current existence we may experience a constant lack of power, suppression of power, manipulation of power, which all become another form of distortion.

As we become more and more conscious of who we are, what our power is and how sacred everything is we begin to remember that we no longer have to play any karmic/distorted realities. We must then clear all the energies, emotions, beliefs that keep these imbalances so we can make more space for our Light to come through. The more Light we hold, the fewer imbalances we have therefore the less karmic realities we play out.

REPAIR

There is a part of the process in which we start to fully remember that we aren't truly broken, we don't have to keep on healing because deep down we are whole and complete in the greater scheme of things. We move from healing into repairing our bodies so that our full Light can fit and fill all of the lack and separation we carry inside. The Light frequencies and codes coming through are what start to recode and repair our DNA so that it comes fully active and functional. Everything in our 3D reality kept our DNA dormant and suppressed in ways that locked us up and erased all of our ancient and sacred memories.

The cellular and DNA repair processes are vast and entails a lot. We start to become more conscious of what we do, what we eat, what we engage in, what we watch so we can recognize what keeps our DNA dormant. We then start to shift things in our reality and we must remove everything that keeps us asleep and closed. This will be challenging at the beginning because of all that we have to change but as you start to open up to your inner guidance you'll start to do "little" steps that will support you in this process. Every step counts no matter how small or insignificant it might seem at first for it will start to create the necessary re-alignments at deeper levels that will open you up to bigger shifts that will completely shift your entire reality.

Physical Reality

Our bodies and fields were programmed in such a way that we had much holes, cords and openings that sucked our energy and Light in more ways than we were consciously aware of. As we become more conscious and open we start to feel more, we start to recognize when our energy starts to drain and deplete. In many instances our reality will also mirror the exact same thing and we start to see leaks, holes, broken down things that need repair. Your entire physical reality will give you clues to what is going on inside so continue to observe everything so that you can go deeper inside and allow your Light to repair what is necessary.

Again our Light codes are the ones that do the cellular and DNA repair but on the physical, emotional and mental plane we must take full responsibility of this and start to fully feel, fully honor and shift, change and repair your physical reality.

Everything in our 3D reality was broken at some level, our relationship with others, our relationship with ourselves, with objects, with our environment, with our emotions and so much more. In order to start repairing all of these we must start to reconnect back with every part of ourselves so that we can resolve and dissolve all the separation that created these distortions. As we reconnect at a deep Soul level we start to have more sacred respect for all that we are and consequently we start to mend everything that was broken. The relationships we have with others and everything around us is only a mere reflection of the relationship or lack thereof that we have with ourselves. The answer lies within for as we continue to establish a more pure, loving and respectful bond with all that we are the more we are able to bring these energies forth in any and every relationship that we have.

COMPLETE

There are many completion phases all throughout this journey. As some end, others just begin and it becomes a continuous flow of many phases that one learns to open up to, appreciate, embrace and honor as it all supports the greater whole. As I began to open up to this journey I realized that not only do we go through LightBody upgrades, recodings, template rewrites and much more but we also go through other types of emotional, mental and physical level of completion when it comes to living in the old world, repeating cycles and breaking free from old perceptions.

LightBody Phases

When big collective energetic portals and passageways open up usually on repeating number days like 01-01 or 01-11 we get flooded with a massive amount of Light frequencies and codes that come through into our field, body, cells and these are the ones that start to recode and reprogram everything. In order to fully allow these frequencies in we have to be fully open and surrender all of our old ego constructs and mentalities so they don't get in the way of this process.

Then we go through the anchoring and full integration of these codes which may activate a template wipe which we then go through ego deaths, deep emotional releases, lightbody upgrades, void spaces, which brings us into zero point. This is just but one of the ways we get to complete one of the many phases and when we reach a full zero point frequency then we must hold it in place inside so that we can re-build, re-create all from this infinite and expansive and pure space.

Your body must go through a complete overhaul of clearing, dissolving, detoxing, purifying and integrating which is very vast and so the more we open up fully and go all in on this journey the more support we will be able to gift our bodies so that we can navigate seamlessly and in a flow that is enjoyable and exciting.

I've seen a lot of people ask if this process will every end and in the greater scheme of things it will never end because it's been always occurring, maybe not at a level where we are physically feeling it like now but our bodies have always gone through their own internal completion phases. What is occurring now is that we are all consciously going through our physical body Ascension process so that we can restore peace and Unity on this planet and continue to expand as Light Beings. We hold the essence of the Universe inside of us and the Universe is always growing, expanding and evolving so at some level we will always continue to shift and change. At the beginning because everything is so weird and bizarre and doesn't conform to anything that we've been taught in the old 3D world and it challenges the ego so much that it is uncomfortable and we don't like it and it's too much for us to deal with but this is normal. Our entire bodies are being reconstructed at a deep cellular level that supports the integrating of our Soul into our physical bodies so that we can live as a Soul here.

As we start to open up to the crazy, weird, illogical, uncomfortable and even painful expansions that occur we will start to remember that this is a very normal, necessary and important part of the process as it is all part of the breaking down of the old constructs. The body is physically dismantling all of the old structures from deep inside and so just like it hurts when we open up our knee or break our nose; the breaking, opening/expanding of our cells in order to bring through more Light is very tangible and sometimes very painful. It you think about it it's like when our bones started to expand and we go through the so called "growing pains", that is exactly what is going on inside of the body. Yes it was painful at times but since we knew or most of us knew what was going on because our parents would tell us we had to just go with the flow and surrender to it. When we become more conscious of what is going on we actually learn to appreciate it and honor it at a deep sacred level and we do anything and everything we are guided to fully support our LightBody in this process.

Mental, Emotional and Physical Completion

The other part of being complete is at a mental, emotional and physical level with any and every part of our 3D reality. There comes a moment where you get so sick, so fed up, so angry, so done with it all that it brings up a powerful energetic force that moves it out in many levels. We will go through deep levels of grief, sadness, anger, rage, frustration, upheaval in order to consciously move, shift, clear this energy out of the body. Sometimes it is just an emotional purge with lots and lots of deep crying, sometimes we need to be more physical and yell, scream, stomp, shake the body uncontrollably, punch a pillow or break something (as appropriately guided of course) so that we can literally let it all out. There has been so much suppressed energy inside at every level that we have no conscious awareness but it's all there.

We have to give ourselves permission to feel it all fully no matter what the emotion is no matter what the body is guiding us to do. When we were growing up we all grew up in a reality where all emotions were not honored, we weren't fully supported in expressing our emotions and so we kept them all inside. Now that we are expanding and becoming more conscious we have to let everything that our inner/separated aspects are still holding inside in an appropriate way so that we can honor these aspects' feelings and emotions in every way.

Anger is a very powerful force, it is an energy that we can utilize to empower ourselves and move out of realities. Anger is a fast moving energy which requires movement and so if we don't fully know how to consciously be angry and move this energy out it can bring a lot of havoc and pain if we utilize this energy in a disrespectful and distorted way that hurts ourselves and others. This is why it is so important to let this energy out on your own, by yourself, in a sacred space where you feel fully loved and honored as you clear this energy. There is an enormous amount of freedom that comes through with this force when we open up and fully honor it and consciously move it out ourselves in a way that is highest aligned for all.

When we fully honor this energy we are able to break free, we are able to open up to our pain, we are able to connect with so many aspects and emotions that were trapped and hidden behind this energy and as this occurs more Light comes through into our bodies balancing and restoring the pure love and peace that we truly are. When you take full responsibility of moving/clearing this energy out yourself without anyone involved you empower yourself in a big way and allows you to not bring an angry aspects of yourself to the table in any situation but instead your highest and most loving version of yourself. The reason why so many of us act or react out of anger is because we have yet to learn how to deal with this energy ourselves, and so it gets triggered by others or by circumstances in light that we may see it, own it and deal/clear it ourselves so that we don't spew it on anyone else.

Completing Contracts

Another huge part of this process is the completion of our karmic contracts. Like mentioned earlier any karmic debt is an imbalance of an energy that we played out in this existence and/or another and we came here to clear and balance fully so that we don't keep recreating this in our reality.

As we become more consciously aware and start to remember more and more of who we truly are and what we are meant to be and do we recognize that we don't need to play any of these karmic contracts anymore. We bring forth this powerful energy of completion forth that can also be felt as a deep emotion of grief, anger or frustration. Feeling and honoring every emotion fully will dissolve all of the cords, ties, attachments, bonds that we had inside of us that kept us bound to that karmic contract. As we consciously dissolve this inside we create a powerful energy that says NO MORE, WE ARE DONE, I AM DONE, I QUIT, I AM FREE, in reference to our old realities. The more we consciously break free from these contracts with the use of this force from a space of purity and love the faster we can break free and balance everything out so we no longer have to endure all of the distorted realities that were created. The reason why we play this karmic realities is because at some level some aspect of ourselves believes that we must fully play our karma in order to balance all of our internal energy when in reality we don't have to physically endure any distorted reality anymore and instead by holding and anchoring and becoming more Light inside we can easily and much faster clear and complete all of these old distorted karmic experiences. In the much more expanded states of consciousness karma doesn't exist because no one is actually a victim here. Everyone chose their respective roles and characters in each existence prior to incarnation based on a Soul contract or agreement. As we become Souls again we consciously choose not to play in the old games of karma, we choose to always come from our highest form of purity, love, peace, Light, unity in every way and in every experience. Remember that if we come from the exacts opposite energies we are playing out a karmic reality and recreating a karmic cycle that keeps us stuck there until we consciously decide to get out.

By being complete in every level and in every way we get to free ourselves in so many different ways that allows us to live a reality as who we truly are; we get to experience and create a world that is filled with the frequencies of peace and unity and as we do we restore Light back into this world.

COMMAND

It took me many years to fully comprehend and deeper innerstand the sacred power behind this word. When I first started to hear this word there was a dissonance inside that I couldn't quite own nor innerstand until much later. There are a lot of cords and ties attached to this frequency that is contracted and restricting. The words control, force and push/pull come into mind when I tune in and there is much distorted frequencies that one must fully clear to open up to this powerful force.

We truly are the commanders of our Light ships, our realities and our world in every aspect whether we are conscious of it or not and as we start to open up to these we start to see/feel/recognize the ins and outs of what we are creating and the purposes for it as well.

When we start to play with this word, we can start to activate our deepest distortions that play around our abuse of power, our control and manipulation. When we were unconscious we believed that things needed to be forced in order to have them, we thought that we weren't worthy of things and so we needed to pull them in an ego distorted way. As we open up to feeling all of these imbalances inside, suppressed emotions and feelings we start to break free from these energies and aspects.

In many ways, you have to continuously dissolve every ego aspect, every control mechanism, every protection structure held deeply inside so that you can start to strip away from the old foundations. We strip ourselves completely bare and naked so we can see our purity, our wholeness, our greatness and as we do there is a frequency of being completely humble that gets activated. We become humble in a pure way, we let go of our old identities, titles and accolades, we become our pure and sacred essence that doesn't need to be on a pedestal, doesn't need to be showy, or loud or offensive, we become quite the opposite, soft, gentle, bright and powerful in a pure loving way. Our energy speaks for us, our essence shines through us, our love is felt in every way the more we continue to hold our Light deeper and deeper inside.

We transform back into the pure states of just being as Light and we start to remember just how sacred this really is. Our Light, our bodies, our thoughts, our emotions become all One and we start to hold a deep level of honor and respect for it all in a way that we have never experienced before. We remember that nothing can break us, nothing can dim us, nothing can kill us for we are everything in every form. As we start to recognize that when we are this pure powerful being we can create an enormous amount of change, beauty, magic, peace and love in so many ways that can truly be felt.

Through this sacred remembrance of who we are we start to activate our deep inner knowing of how to create things, how to materialize things and how to command things. It can be as simple as opening up your heart, mind, field and body and just allowing the frequencies that will support you in bringing forth what it is that you are calling forth that is highest aligned with your Soul, journey, LightBody and mission. This is a way of commanding things forth in a gentle kinda of way. Of course there are countless ways in which we do this and we just have to be open to them all.

We can alchemize deep emotions in a way that supports this

too. Anger is a great activator of pure power in many ways and so if we can consciously feel the anger, honor it, unanchor from it and dissolve it we can create a force, a Soul drive and desire that opens us up to the systems that we need to hold in order to materialize things in our reality. Remember that the creation and manifestation comes as easy as you thinking it, saying it or desiring it. We then have to hold the structures and systems in place inside of our bodies so that we can allow ourselves to open/expand big enough to receive it in the physical as an actually tangible experience.

The Journey

As you open up and embrace this journey you will start to realize just how important, sacred it truly all is where nothing precedes it. The journey of re-discovery, the path to self mastery, the way of ascension is what we are here to be and do and so we start to consciously remove anything and anyone that distracts, impeded or is out of alignment with all of this. As this occurs we start to open up for more things to show up that will support us. In the beginning it might be spontaneous or miraculous how these things start showing up in your reality sometimes without even knowing that you needed them and its way cool. You then start to open up to the frequencies that support you instead of the tangible things or objects because we start to realize that by just holding the frequencies in place inside all "out there" becomes tangible and physical. We start to focus less on the physical and rather on the energetic side of things because that is where the key resides. Before we were so focused on the physical, material objects and we paid no attention to the energy involved behind it.

As you open up to your feelings, feeling them fully and releasing them you start to activate more of the pure frequencies of love, peace, joy that open up portals inside for things to come through. Our Universe is infinite, expansive and all-knowing and so if we just hold on to the frequency and open completely up we become a match for amazing things to pop up.

This is another powerful way to command; becoming the frequencies and holding the field in place for everything you need that will support you in your mission, path and service work will magically appear in ways that you couldn't see before.

BELIEVE

The belief frequency is one that holds much power and deeply anchors structures in place. It is said that what you belief is what you end up creating in your reality whether you are conscious of it or not. The beliefs you have about yourself, others, the world, your reality, your "past", etc., create a great bond that keep you recreating experiences that reinforce that believe whether it is and old earth belief or a New Earth/Higher Consciousness one. Each belief that you have connects with a grid, a system of mathematical equations naked to the human eye or linear mind that create the foundational structures in which that reality sits on. Many of us have deeply unconscious and subconscious beliefs that we have no clue we have. Whether these beliefs have been engrained at a very early age, absorbed through our experiences/surroundings or brought into the body across multiple dimensions and other existences we all must become aware of them so that we can learn/remember how to shift them ourselves.

Keep in mind that it doesn't really matter what the belief is, what truly matter is the frequency that it holds because that is what essentially needs to be cleared. The words we attach to this frequency is just a way in which we have learned to describe or label something so that we can explain it to others but in the end it is important to evolve out of the judgment that words can carry and connect with the frequency of it. It is in connecting to the frequency that we can start to feel the heaviness, the discord, the imbalance that it is creating inside of our bodies and therefore in our entire reality.

As we begin to open up to the feeling, the emotion that is brought forth from the awareness of a deep rooted belief inside, we start unhinge and unanchor and dissolve all structures and systems. This is a continual process, a constant awareness of your entire reality and observing what old beliefs everything is tied to. The key is to start opening up to this practice, open up to knowing more and open up to feeling everything that this new awareness will bring up and activate. It is integral that we allow ourselves to feel everything, no matter how ugly, distorted, "horrible" and bad we believe that belief to be. Again it doesn't truly matter for we must remember that we all have these core beliefs so it doesn't make us any less, or unworthy by recognizing or owning that we have such said beliefs.

Changing Beliefs

When we awaken and start to remember that there is more to this reality, mostly none of the beliefs we have been instilled with resonate anymore. They don't feel true inside, and we begin to feel the heaviness of it all. We start to remember that we are not the small, weak, fragile, powerless beings that need to be told what to do and protected but quite the opposite. We then start the journey of letting go of the old belief systems and opening up to new ones.

Every single belief that held the 3D reality in place has to be completely removed and dissolved from our entire body/field/reality. This also takes a huge amount of commitment on our part but it is what we came here to do and accomplish.

The Evolution

There is something fascinating that I've learned from my own Ascension guide, Lisa Transcendence Brown, about belief systems and how we evolve out of them. As we open up to new ones, ones that are fully in alignment with our pure Light and love we start to hold a different energy inside. We start to move from beliefs to a value system, a system that fully supports us, fully loves us, and fully re-aligns us with everything that we are. The value system is similar to a deep inner knowing inside. Evolving from "I believe" in something or someone to "I know" without a doubt in my Soul that this is possible is a much more powerful frequency. This is what we are evolving into, not just a belief in the unseen or etheric but a deep connection with it that it becomes part of our sacred knowing.

Having a belief in something infers that something could be true or untrue; someone else can have a different belief and therefore creating separation and segregation at some level. We are moving out of this system also because our personal truths change in every moment, we can want or need something at this moment and then want something else in the next. Our realities become a free quantum flow in every way where we don't affix or attach to anything. Our core value systems are less rigid and stiff like the old belief systems were. Yes, we are moving into a value system where all beings and energy is valued, honored, respected, embraced and loved in every way. These new value systems are based on Cosmic and Universal Laws that are set on Unity Consciousness.

The values that we had when we were closed and unconscious are completely opposite of the ones we have as we ascend into higher levels of consciousness. We start to value ourselves, our Light, our LightBody, our journey, our purity above all because we know without a doubt who we are and what we are and what we bring forth by valuing our selves above all. In the old realities we would focus on the outside, on the material gains, on other people, on the titles and accomplishments because we thought and believed that that was what life was about and that if we would focus on that we would be fulfilled. The more we start to shift our focus towards ourselves, our internal world, our Soul/heart and all that we are we start to remember that none of that actually brought what we once thought it would.

What you value is huge and it is what we become. It moves away from a belief system because that is what old systems and foundations like religions were based on and it created much separation in this world. We must move away from what we believe to be true or who we believe to be right and rather focus on the pure essence that we all hold inside regardless of what our belief system is. All of the old systems are collapsing more and more because we know that it doesn't bring peace and unity but quite the opposite and so as we move away from these systems ourselves and collapse them at a deep internal level we get to completely dismantle them and we start to rebuild a whole new world where Unity Consciousness is the foundation of everything.

Continue to open up to the ALL new through the anchoring of your Light. Your Light will show you the way and will assist you in remembering what is truly valuable, what supports you as Light and how to live in a whole new way.

RESTORE

The process of ascension is a restoring, a returning of who we are and who we've always been deep down in our core. For many the illusion of separation is still quite strong where they perceive the systems "out there" to be separate from who they are and what they hold. This is about remembering that we programmed this reality in the way that it is. Consciousness takes many, many forms and as Creator Beings we create many things in order to experience ourselves from many different angles and many forms. Many times we've played in the distortions of separation creating much havoc in the Universe and other planets. As one of the many purposes that we came down here for is to fully clear all of these existences and restore back the planet and ourselves to our original state of consciousness.

We must be fully opened so we can remember more and more of our many purposes on this planet. Releasing judgment towards the 3D systems, the old establishment, the elite and everything that controlled, suppressed and manipulated the masses is a beyond crucial part of this process. There are many emotions that we have to honor and feel about everything that has been going on in the 3D realms and no longer get sucked in. The ego loves to play in the old, the drama, the trauma, the "I'm right you're wrong" game, battle, competition, pain and so much more and it isn't until we fully feel all these emotions and connect with all the aspects still playing in the game that we come to truly free ourselves. What we perceive to be playing "out there" is what is actually playing out inside in every dimensional existence. In order to shift it we must be willing to dive deeper than we've ever gone and allowed ourselves to go so that we can see from a much more expanded perception. All the control, manipulation, distortion is a frequency we all hold inside, in fact we had to agree to hold these structures inside our physical body in order to incarnate down into this realm so we can shift everything from inside. Remember that as Souls we all chose this reality, we all chose the experience, the people, the circumstances because we knew that it would support us in the long run as/when we begin to awaken and remember. When you move from the old mentality of separation and victimhood you start to empower yourself in ways that free you and support you in restoring back your Light.

Becoming Whole

The Light we are starting to open up to is what restores us back to having a Higher and more expanded level of consciousness. Our dense/heavy bodies cannot operate in the higher realms because there is no space for the Light to sustain itself in this field. We have to purge everything that is heavy and that holds the frequencies of separation so that we can have the necessary space to hold, anchor, sustain and become our pure Light.

As we all do this we start to restore everything around us, everything that was out of place, out of Soul alignment and out of balance must be shifted in a way that fully supports our Light. This takes conscious participation in every level and from every aspect of our being as all plays an integral part and is part of the whole picture. As we move our personal reality our "external" reality starts to shift as well. Not only does this occur at an energetic level but also at a physical level. The 3D reality becomes so far removed from your world in order for you to continually re-build a whole new one from scratch where purity, peace and balance is restored in every way.

It's important to remember that the challenges that occur all along the way are important. They are part of what you chose in order to continue to see more, feel more and make the necessary choices that will restore your bravery and courage as you boldly move out of the old realms.

As we move more and more out of the old realms we start to achieve more peace and balance within that always our entire body/system/field to become fully restored and capable of holding our Light. All of our aspects, Soul fragments and parts of ourselves that were separated, ostracized, abandoned, marginalized and left behind now start to fully open and return back home, back into the purity of our hearts.

It is in this restoration of our entire body/field/world that we get to restore the Light and our planet will be what it once was, a place where everyone is honored, supported, embraced, loved and unified as One.

BREATHE

Breathe. Our own breath is so key in this process. Becoming conscious of our breath reconnects us to our heart space and to our body in ways that assist us in noticing if anything is off inside. We have forgotten just how powerful our breath is because we do it so automatic, without thinking, without being conscious as if it weren't important at all. And yet it is, our breath is part of what allows us to be in flow, what keeps us alive and what allows us to inhale more Light.

The breath can be utilized in many, many ways throughout this process so remember there is no "right or wrong" way of doing it because it all assists in some level. When we start going through the emotional passageway and a lot of our deepest most suppressed emotions start coming up to the surface it can get really intense physically and emotionally. If you open up to your breath and allow it to assist you by reconnecting with it you will notice what a huge difference this can do. Just by being with the breath can greatly support you because the breath has the capacity to bring you back to your center, calm you and recalibrate you in more ways than we can innerstand.

Working with the Breath

Like previously mentioned there are many ways and practices nowadays that can assist you in this path and so whichever one you are guided towards in that moment is perfect. The simplest and most easiest way to start is by simply closing your eyes, putting your hand over your heart and becoming conscious of the breath. Listen to it, notice your body's movements as you inhale and exhale, relax your muscles more if you feel any tension, fully surrender to this moment and become fully present with YOU. It is about becoming one with the breath, becoming unified in this harmonic flow of the inhale and exhale that supports your inner world to also be at one with this flow. In this state you can open up to doing much more like start reconnecting with different parts of your body, open your inner vision to receive guidance and messages, allow your body/field to expand, fly and float. Consciously intending to breathe in more Light into your vessel will support in clearing/dissolving any heaviness, blockages or tightness. The list is truly endless, you can do so much in this space and the more that you do it the more that will come through for you that can assist you if you are open to it. If thoughts are coming through, that is ok, you want to be with the thoughts as well instead of suppressing them or controlling them for the thoughts give you a lot of information about what you are still holding inside that you may or may not be conscious about. Remember that thoughts are just energy, they need to flow and they need an outlet and so the more that you open up to them, honor them for what they are trying to show you and let them float away and dissolve the less and less those thoughts will come through.

Breathing can bring us back into that stillness, that presence, that zero point field and make us One with everything. It can reconnect us with parts of ourselves and parts of our bodies that were so far removed from our consciousness so that we can bring through the energy that is needed to allow everything to be restored and balanced inside.

Breathing stands alone so you don't necessarily have to engage in a specific form of practice or meditation to simply work with it. In fact the more we connect with our breath in any and every way the more we become One with it; this will allow us to become more conscious of the messages that it wants to bring forth. Yes, your breath can change depending on the situation you're in, what you're feeling, what is going on inside of you and becoming more conscious of this will assist you in listening to the body so that you can start to learn more about yourself.

Shifting Dimensions

Your breathing will change as you start to move and shift into higher levels of consciousness and dimensions. Each dimension has its own frequency bandwidth and so our physical body has to upgrade in many ways in order to sustain itself in the higher dimensions. Breathing is one of the ways in which you can tell when you are shifting and raising your overall frequency for it will feel weird and bizarre. You may feel like you can't breathe sometimes, or you cannot take a full deep breath and other sensations may also come up. I can agree that it is interesting to say the least when you're going through it because it is such a different sensation than what we are used so it's important to not fear it and to be open to it. The way that I have seen it for myself, it's almost like trying to grasp for breath right before you go underwater but instead of going underwater imagine the water level rising and rising on you so it's like you have to grasp for breath constantly until the water levels stay constant and you are able to take a deeper breath. Another way to see it is like if you were to go hiking at an extremely high altitude than what your body is used, the density of the air is much thinner and so it may be harder to breath and so you may have to slow down your body and your movements to adjust to it. This is exactly what is happening and your body needs to adapt, adjust and acclimate to the level of density that is present in the higher realms. So even though you may not be physically climbing a mountain, you are raising your frequency so much that you start to reach higher dimensions and your body will feel it. I know, pretty crazy, and in fact this whole process is crazy and cool all at the same time when you truly open to it and embrace it.

This will become easier especially as you become more conscious of when it's happening and you go with your body's flow. Remember that we are going to keep going higher and higher in dimensions and so we will need to continue to acclimate to the higher frequencies so that our bodies can stabilize at a deeper and deeper level.

Keep listening to your body, supporting it by not giving into the fear of the unknown and bizarre and you'll start to see how your body adapts and adjusts much more easily.

SHARE

Your Light is meant to be shared, it is meant to radiate and shine Bright because that is what Light does. However coming down into the density of the third dimensional realms of consciousness we start to see and experience that being our Light is not appreciated, understood, valued, embraced, accepted and so many other things. We start to learn how to behave in order to receive these things and many times it is opposite of being our Light. So we grow up in a survival mode where doing anything we needed to do in order to be loved and accepted was more important than being ourselves. So we start to dim, suppress, hide, fear and even hate our own Light. We became someone that we are not, putting on masks, faking it until we "make it" and sucking it up. This has gone too deep that now with all the Light that is coming through the planet our Light can no longer be hidden. These Light encoded frequencies are triggering everything that has buried our Light deep inside of us, from deep unresolved emotions, suppressed feelings, old belief systems about who we are and so much more. They are showing us all the energies we've been stuffing inside of ourselves that has kept us from showing up as Light and sharing it.

We can no longer hide from our Light, our bodies can no longer sustain the amount of heaviness we have subjected it to in order to survive and now it is doing everything it can to support us in clearing, cleansing and activating more Light.

We have to open up to our Light, remind ourselves that it is safe being our Light and no longer fear it. Of course this is not an overnight process and there is much to it but when you consciously commit to open up your heart, your mind and your body to your Light powerful things start to occur. Your Light is hear to heal/repair/dissolve all the separation still held inside, there is no reason to fear it anymore but to embrace it for it is you. We've always been this Light but our concept of what Light is doesn't quite fit in the belief system that all of us were taught from. This is about breaking free from these old systems, not believing in them, not supporting them, not feeding them and giving ourselves permission to go all in on our self discovery journey.

Learning to not fear our Light, takes conscious commitment on every level. We were trained to fear ourselves without being consciously aware of it and it is in the continual reconnection with all that we are from a sacred space of being and not of judgment that we start to see all that we are and all that we've been. None of what we've ever done, said or experienced truly matters in the bigger scheme of things because nothing can every change who we truly are. Our Light is unbreakable, unshakeable and undeniably powerful in every way and so the more and more we start to remember this the more we start to honor ourselves and the more we start to share from a space of purity.

Purity of Intention

Our Light is meant to be shared and seen in every way because in this sharing is how we start to activate codes of remembrances in others so *they* can start to remember this for themselves too. If we don't become our Light and always bring it to the table then we will continue to play in the game of unconsciousness where we hide and suppress who we are and others as well. As we start to open up more and more we start to see where we are still hiding our Light, who we are still hiding our Light from, and how this influences our reality. There are many people in our reality that we chose to play a certain role that would test us and challenges us to no longer fear our Light, to no longer suppress our Light and to start sharing our Light even when it feels scary and daunting and dangerous. Others in our reality will fully hold the space we need in order to feel comfortable being our Light and sharing our Light. It is important to honor these both types of people that are in our reality because they serve a very important purpose in our journey.

As you start to open up to every person in your reality you will no longer dim your Light for fear that it threatens other people or even your space. We start to remember that our Light must not be dimmed because if we do then we make room for our ego aspects to come through and when they do they create an emotion that is rooted in an unresolved emotion, fear-lack based mentality. When we dim our Light we give away our power, we close our heart and we become small and weak. However this is not who we are meant to be and definitely not what we came here to do in this world but quite the opposite. We came here to remember and to remind everyone of who we truly are, of how loved and wanted we are, how safe being our pure self is as this will restore peace on this planet. The way we do this is by returning to our pure Light and shining it in every way so that we can elevate our consciousness and no longer feed into the hate, fear, lack, suppression, battle and old ways.

Sharing in Service

As we continue to become our pure essence as Light we start to activate our service codes. These service codes are part of our many Soul purposes and missions that we agreed to fulfill before ever incarnating here. The more we anchor our Light and become our Light the more we are responsible for shining and sharing our Light in every way.

Each individual person came here to shine their Light in their own unique way, through their own gifts and talents. In order to do this we must strip away all of the old ego constructs which shared from fear and lack. The old world is about competing and battling, seeing who's better than, who's worthy, who's number 1 and all of these structures that kept us believing that we weren't good enough just as we are and so we needed to prove it by winning or accomplishing something.

The Light that we are doesn't need to prove anything to anyone, we don't need to compete to gain recognition or approval, we don't need to battle with anyone and compare with others because our pure strength doesn't align with any of the old beliefs of what strength is. As Light we are infinite and we hold an enormous amount of power that comes from purity and love. It's always been this and it will remain this for eternity, nothing will ever change that.

Moving away from the old will allow us to exist as pure beings where we can support one another, uplift, inspire, assist, encourage, embrace and love in every way possible. We share our Light because it brings all of these energies to the table and the more that we do this the more we get to recreate a whole new world that are fully aligned with these core foundations.

The more we share our Light, the more information we spread all around the globe which will continuously activate more and more Souls to remembering their deep inner essence and value. This is everyone's service roles, no matter how you are guided to share your Light. For some it will be through dancing, writing, painting, it doesn't matter for what matters is that you allow yourself to engage in that which adds more Light to your life because it will also add more Light to others and hence the entire world.

One fascinating aspect about sharing your Light is that not only does it activate others but it also activates you at a deeper and deeper level. The more codes you share in whatever way you are guided to activates new templates and structures so that this act becomes a new way of existing, a new way of being that is completely different from the old. We want to anchor deeper and deeper and even deeper levels of our Soul/Light inside continuously so that we can evolve fully out of the third dimensional realm of consciousness and just keep ascending higher and higher into new worlds and new levels that completely eradicate the old.

Sharing is a powerful force indeed and the more you open yourself up you'll start to remember that this is part of just being who you are and that act alone will change your entire reality and the entire world.

PLAY

  The frequency of play is so powerful throughout this journey, especially in the moments when it gets rough and tough. When we were young we lived to play, to have fun, to sing and laugh and then a lot of a sudden we got to a point where we might have felt like we couldn't do it anymore, we weren't allowed to or we weren't supposed to based on our linear age or the societal expectations that we get drowned in. Life then gets stripped away from play, from the pure fun and our Light gets sucked away in the hustle and bustle of the day to day of adulthood.

  It is now more than ever that we are starting to open up and realize that the way our 3D realities have been set up to be are no fun, of course there might be some fun but deep down we know it's not what we want anymore, or what we expected or maybe it's just not fulfilling anymore to follow a 9-5 routine and not have space to enjoy life with the things that truly matter.

  So how do we actually break free from the old and play again? It is all a constant choice in every moment and it can be as simple as choosing to bring more play into your life. If we open up our minds and our hearts we can bring the magic of play in every moment and break free from the old ties and chains. It is our minds that keep us enslaved at some level from believing that we don't have a choice, that this is the only way, that if I let go and run astray we won't be able to survive or be supported and yet all of this is just a perception. There are many perceptions to everything and if you choose to keep believing that then nothing will stay the same but if you choose to open up just a little bit and a little bit more and a little bit more you'll start to see just how many opportunities you actually have in choose something different.

When we choose to bring the element/frequency of play into our daily lives we are able to be in this pure flow that guides us and leads us in ways that are fun, magical and blissful. We aren't so tight up or stressed about things because when we are in this frequency everything else dissolves and we get to remember that there is always room for change, there is always a solution to everything and nothing is ever fixed. Only if we stay in our linear minds do we get trapped and sucked in believing that there is no way out, there is no freedom, there is no choice but to keep stuck in the old ways. Venture inside, take yourself deeper into your being, your Soul, your body and start to reconnect with the inner child, that child that is yearning to come out and play, the one that wants so much to reconnect with you and feel the love and support from YOU.

The Inner and Divine Child

We've had this inner child trapped inside, we locked him up, we took away all of its toys and games, all the fun and play and it just slowly started to fade away the more we got sucked into the rules and expectations of others as we become older. It is time to set him/her free so that we can reconnect with this aspect and activate all the magic we have inside so that he/she feels safe enough to come back out and play.

Every inner child aspect that was ever hurt, wounded, traumatized is the part of us that is separated, it ran away from home and it gets activated every time something or someone triggers any old wound, unresolved emotion and suppressed memory. When we open up to feeling all the emotions that this child still has deep inside we open up a door for all of that to actually be released, we give ourselves the opportunity to not carry that heaviness any more and we allow more Light, peace and a deep innerstading to come through. As each inner child aspect starts to open up more and feel everything through us and our bodies they start to merge with our pure essence, they unify back inside and they return to living in the purity of our heart. It is then when the Divine Child starts to emerge, this pure aspect of our child starts to come through in every way. We get to rebirth ourselves into this Higher Self aspect where we get to re-learn how to exist from this purity and love, we get to create a whole new reality for ourselves that is filled with magic and joy and fun because we have a deep knowing and remembrance that these energies are all part of who we are. Our linear age doesn't matter at all for isn't about that, it's about breaking free from the old 3D rules that told us we couldn't play anymore and allowing ourselves to be in the frequency that we are because in that we recognize just how simpler life is, how much fun and joy we get to have and how we are able to transform not just our reality but the world at large.

Clearing Distortions of Play

It is important to go through feeling and releasing all of the distorted beliefs we have about play. There are some moments where we use or used play from a separated place inside. Sometimes we keep ourselves hiding behind the energy of play so that we don't take responsibility for the things that we must shift and re-align in our lives. As powerful as play is we have to recognize where are we utilizing it to keep ourselves away from feeling and recognizing the things that are keeping us tight and locked up inside and when we can bring more of this pure energy that can add more Light into our life.

All of us at some level did not get to fully play when we were little, we were told when to play and when to stop, we were told how to play and who to play with and this all created a lot of emotions inside that at the time we probably didn't have permission to feel fully. All of these deeply suppressed emotions are keeping the energy of play at bay, we might be angry that others get to play, we might be judging ourselves because we can't play, we might be grieving inside for all the times we weren't allowed to play. Every single one of these experiences must be fully felt from a core level so that you can start to free yourself from the heaviness of it all.

Open up your heart to clearing everything you may still have lingering towards play that may keep you closed off to it. The more you free yourself from these energies the more you'll start to see and find the joy, beauty and magic that play offers and you'll start to feel at peace with it in every way.

OBSERVE

We become very observant of our reality because we remember that everything that is around us, everything inside of us holds keys and codes that are meant to activate us at a deeper level. Becoming the observer of absolutely everything without holding judgment or polarity is key. When we start to focus/open to our whole reality we start to have access to things/information that we didn't have before. The 3D realms of consciousness keep one distracted, focusing on problems, fear and lack, it kept us from opening up because we believed that the "outer world" was bigger/stronger and so we always had to be closed, guarded and protected.

When we start to hold the frequency that we are as Light we start to feel the essence of how infinite, expansive and powerful we truly are. We start to remember that we are Source Creator in its entirety. There is not one aspect of our reality that we don't create whether we are conscious of it or not, whether we believe it or not, it doesn't matter. As creators the more we start to see/observe everything around us the more we start to feel the energy the more we will be able to recognize the energy that is activating or triggering inside. Everything that is around us is a vibrational match to what we hold inside and as we open up to it we start to recognize where its coming from; where is it being created from, what emotion is it attached to, what belief is it feeding, and much more.

The body can tell us so much the more we open up to it and when we open up to asking these sorts of questions it will gladly tell us the more we listen to it. This is a constant process for everything that was part of our 3D reality was deeply embedded in our physical body and fed/supported the energies of fear, separation, not good enough, blame, shame and so many other heavy emotions. What ends up happening is that because we have suppressed all of these at deep unconscious and subconscious levels we learned to disconnect completely from ourselves but still function in our 3D daily lives. Now the body is becoming activated with so much Light that it wants to create more space for it so that the body doesn't continue to carry all the excess weight that is preventing the natural and organic flow of all body systems.

When we open up to our bodies we will start to feel more and although it can be an extremely emotional experience at times it is a necessary part of the process to set ourselves free. The more we start to feel inside the more our senses become more open and activated and so as we continue to observe our reality our senses will start to give us more signs, messages, triggers that will show us what role that "outside" thing is playing in our reality; is it supporting our Light or is it dimming it, is it creating more peace or more chaos, is it binding us to the old or supporting us in creating the NEW. All of these things must come into our awareness so that we can start to make the necessary choices that we need in order to re-align EVERYTHING in our reality to that which supports our peace and unity.

Non-Judgment

There is so very much to see in everything because everything holds a key, a purpose in our roles and in our realities. One of the reasons why many of us didn't want to see is because we didn't like what we saw, we didn't love what was "out there", we would much rather turn our heads, run away from it, separate from it or pretend that it's not there. And yet all of these choices were part of what created more of what we didn't like/want to see in our world. You see how running away and not wanting to see creates this energetic pull that actually keeps us bound to it and re-creates it over and over in our reality so we can finally own up to it, see it and not fear it? This is KEY. We must not flee from what we fear because that will only grow bigger and stronger and one of the purposes of that is so that we can open up and remember that we are not less or smaller than that "out there", in fact we created it, yes we created it all from the beliefs, emotions, thoughts that we still hold inside that we don't want to see and feel and release. Everything we see "outside" is deeply connected to all that we are and have been and when we open up to it we open up a key door that allows us not just the freedom we yearn but the power to shift, change and re-create it.

Nothing perceived to be "out there" can ever be bigger than you because it is you. If somewhere inside of you feels like you need to protect from that "out there" it is only because *that* is playing an aspect of yourself that you fear. When you fear something you become small and powerless because you believe it is separate than you, but the fear is only a frequency, it is an energy that when felt and honored sets you completely free and as you do you start to believe in yourself again, you start to remember that you are more powerful than you thought and that you created that to assist you in remembering exactly *that*.

If you can recognize and just observe when you are holding judgment towards anything in your reality and then bring it back inside and see, what aspect of myself am I judging? What part of that thing or person don't I like and is it representing an aspect of something that I once was or wanted to be? The people in your reality are either going to be an aspect of your lower self (separated/ego) or your Higher Self (Soul/purity). Many times we call forth people in our reality that mirror aspects of ourselves that are still unresolved, wounded, traumatized and playing ego/mind separation. Start to recognize what emotion they are triggering inside and what aspects of myself are still holding on to that belief/experience/emotion. The more you can start to feel/observe and reconnect with these aspects the more you start to dissolve all the frequencies and cords that kept you tied to that reality. This will be extremely freeing in many levels and it will allow you to create a reality where the people around you aren't triggering you and you aren't judging them. You can literally have a different experience with that same person based on all that you allow yourself to clear from a deeper and deeper level inside.

The more you unify inside the more you start to connect with everyone in a deeper level and you remember that they are only an aspect of yourself and as you start to honor, love and embrace yourself you will start to have the same feeling towards everything and everyone around you because you'll remember that noting "outside" of yourself is against you, it is just trying to show you something about yourself. In that awareness and deep sacred Soul remembrance we get to respect, honor, appreciate everything and everyone in our world and we get to utilize our creator powers to shift, re-align anything and everything inside so that we can experience the full on magic, beauty and peace in every way, in every level and with others in our reality.

INTENT

      We are always making intentions whether we are conscious of it or not. When I awakened I started to learn more about intentions and how they work. All my life I had been making intentions but I wasn't fully conscious of it. In the old world we start by setting goals, having dreams and vision boards and yet it goes much deeper than that. Our intentions come from our core, from what we hold inside for this is what makes the intention pure or impure. Because of how much fear and lack we had inside our physical body most of our intentions came from fear and lack and weren't pure. Before when the world was denser we could survive, sustain and even thrive in spite of having impure intentions but now as more and more Light enters the planet this is no longer possible. We have to return to full consciousness so that we can see all that we have created from fear and lack so we can dismantle it and recreate from the pure place that is inside of our higher heart.

      Everything from our jobs, relationships, material gains, identities and more were created based on the societal imprint that we had to be this or that in order to survive, be accepted and wanted. We thought going to school, getting a high paying job, becoming famous and even having a family was going to be what made us whole and happy and now more than ever we are starting to remember that there is more to life than all of this.

Our reality starts to look very different when we start to open our hearts and minds to the fact that there is much more to what we believed. We start to remember dreams and desires we've always had or used to have when we were growing up. When we were kids we remembered more and so a lot of the things we were passionate about were actually one of the many Soul purposes and missions we came to fulfill here on this planet. Now this is coming back circle for many of us and we are returning to this, we are activating more and more Light inside that is supporting us in creating a fulfilled life that we knew we could have when we were growing up.

Pure Intentions

As we anchor more Light inside of our bodies we start to become more of our pure love and power. We start to align all of our thoughts with who we truly are and our intentions start to shift. We no longer start creating and intending based on the belief that we are weak and unworthy but rather from a place inside where we know we are whole and enough... yes we truly are enough to do, be, have everything we want that is highest aligned with our Soul.

In the old days we used to believe that we could have anything we wanted even those things that fed our ego lack and fear based mentalities but now things are greatly changing. When our needs, wants and desires aren't pure then they aren't supporting our Soul and therefore they won't serve the world, in fact they are only creating more lack, pain and suffering in this world. We must be willing to really dive deep inside and see/feel where we are coming from when we want something. Are we feeding the ego or are we feeding the Soul? The ego desires will be opposite from that of the Soul and they will feed suppressed emotions, lack based mentalities, victimhood, control and other energies that keep us bound to the old. The Soul is nourished through everything that is Light, pure, peaceful, joyful, harmonious and loving in every way. This is where we must all create from and no longer give in to what our ego wants.

The more we hold the purity of our heart the more we will want to have/create that which supports our Soul and uplifts the world. Deep down we aren't bad beings for creating such separation we were just so unconscious that we didn't know any better. The more conscious we become the more we intent to create and have things that benefit the greater good of all and we no longer hold value towards the things that are praised and honored in the old 3D realities. Our entire life and value system changes and as it does so does the entire collectives.

Keep allowing your Light to come through and shift everything that is heavy and distorted so that everything you say, do, have and desire becomes part of a Soul expression that brings more peace and harmony to the world.

MOVE/WALK/JUMP

We have grown accustomed to leading stagnant, static and sedentary lives. A lot of our reality has been molded and structures to make things accessible in ways where we don't have to move, walk or pause and in many cases we are told when, how and why to do certain things. We are bombarded with so many rules and regulations that don't support the natural flow of the body. Times are changing though where more of us are starting to feel it, our bodies are starting to feel it, our whole being is getting the itch, the calling, the pull to start moving more in whatever forms we are being guided to.

The natural physiological structure of the body was meant for us to move, sway, jump and be free but yet when we live in a way that it doesn't support this our bodies become heavier and heavier and heavier. The stagnation causes a lot of density that creates many imbalances in the body which lead to many body conditions. It's time to listen to our bodies more, really start to remember what our bodies were built for and create a reality that fully supports that. If any part of your reality doesn't support the movement and flow of your physical body then it is going to be up to each and every single one of us to start making the necessary changes that will fully honor the body.

Everything is held inside of our physical structures, our emotions, our thoughts, our desires, our physical realities, everything. It is the house that holds the foundation of our world and when you start to put the two and two together you realize just how important your body actually is.

Walking allows us to move out of one location to another; it doesn't matter whether you have physical legs or not this applies to all. This simple movement is huge and can be utilized in many ways and for many things. Our bodies are meant to move, shift, change location, because we are energy as such it is part of our innate being. Sometimes we like to believe that we sitting/being in one place is enough, or much more comfortable, or even easier and yet deep down it is not what we are. As energy beings we are meant to move, we are meant to fly, float, turn, jump because this is a natural flow of all things and when we are able to move in perfect harmony with everything we create a simple and harmonious reality/experience as well. Because we are not meant to be stagnant and paralyzed it is actually harder on ourselves and on our bodies to not move, it literally goes against our nature.

There is however a phase of the journey in which we do sit still in order to be with all that we are. We sometimes used movement, being busy all the time because we were avoiding or running away from the things we were feeling and therefore didn't want to deal with them. When you open yourself to sit with them even if it might be a bit uncomfortable at first you are allowing yourself to feel more of that which created a force inside that made you too afraid to move and do the choices that you knew would be more in alignment with your Soul.

All the heaviness inside pulls us down to where it is more challenging to walk or move and so as we navigate this process we come to realize that we must be able to move the heaviness of what's inside so we can move and walk with so much more ease.

The heaviness of all of the thoughts, memories, emotions, beliefs and programs keep us bound to one place, one location, one perspective, one reality and the more we continue to hold on to them the harder and harder it will be to move. For many of us the body is speaking louder than ever before, showing us, telling us where these heavy blocks are in the body so that we can become conscious of them and start to break them down, dissolve them, feel them and honor them. This creates more freedom in every level not just in the inside but also in the "outside."

The more our body starts to break free from the limitations that were held inside in our cells and DNA so much comes forth that supports us in our ability to move, walk and jump again. We start to feel the flow of our bodies, we start to move with the rhythm of our Soul, we start to go deeper in our own inner journey, we start to remember what we've been missing and how this movement is part of what we are meant to be and do. In the old world our realities conformed with the old paradigms that created fear of moving, fear of being ourselves and even fear of wanting change. There are thousands and millions of people all over the planet right now that are finally waking up to wanting change and we must continuously remind ourselves that it all starts within. Nothing is every meant to be forced or push because then if we do this then we wouldn't be allowing others to be free and it would go against the very thing that we want and the thing that we are.

Becoming free in every way starts is by freeing ourselves first, letting go of our own conceived and perceived limitations in every level and in every part of our bodies. The less limitations we have the less resistance we have to making the personal changes that we are being called to do. This allows us to actually become that which we want to see and experience in our world. The more and more we remember this and live this way the more magnificent and powerful shifts we are going to create in every part of our world and the entire planet as a whole.

Quantum Jumping

As we continue to break free from all that was stuck, stagnant, hidden, suppressed and painful at an emotional, mental, physical and energetic level we are going to do some major quantum jumping. The term quantum jumping is basically jumping but at a quantum/cellular/DNA level. Because all is energy and everything at its core is energy when you are able to shift/change/transform things at the quantum/energetic level we get to completely transcend and move further and farther away from what we once knew. This includes people, relationships, locations, careers, material objects, everything. Nothing stays the same, we move equally as fast as Light speed itself and we get to move our reality in ways that are virtually impossible by old human standards. Sometimes these jumps might be perceived through "small", silent, subtle changes but they are far from it. Anything that is changed at a deep quantum/DNA level is massive, it is more than what our linear minds can innerstand and yet this is a normal part of our capabilities as we continue to become true to our form.

These quantum jumps are amazing and fascinating and it's important to remember that they do take a lot to hold and maintain. Our entire being will be pushed, challenged, tested in many ways as we move through our physical reality and observe what has to go and what stays, what is no longer aligned and what still is, what we need to be, do, bring, remove and add to our reality in order to sustain the energetic shift of the quantum jump.

Our entire reality now has to fit and fully re-align in every way so that we can maintain the new reality that is being birth through this jump. More things will be revealed, we may have to go and feel deeper levels of our being, our whole physical structures have to go through a deep purge, detox, cleanse and purification process at a deeper level than before so that it can create the necessary space in order to allow the new gridding structures to come through. So all in all, get ready because quantum jumping up levels you in a whole new way but I know deep down we are all ready for this because these are the changes that we all have to be open to and allowing in every part of our reality for the big massive changes to occur in our world. So keep going and keep allowing those quantum jumps to occur in every way.

MOVE/SING/DANCE

Continuing the flow of how we are all beings that move, singing and dancing become part of our new realities in many ways. Singing and dancing become the physical expression of the harmony, symphony and free flow that we truly are. Because of all the density that we had to agree to carry in order to come down into this physical realm we suppressed ourselves in many ways from being able to sing and dance.

There is an over infatuation with how things should look, feel, sound, taste, move, be, smell and all based on the 3D structures that basically set the standards which let's not forget we allowed and created ourselves. So we all grow up thinking and believing that if we don't meet the societal standards we are not good enough and if we are not good enough then we shouldn't even attempt or try to engage in things we aren't good at. In some ways many of us have broken free from some of these rules, some are now starting too and others are at some level still continuing to support them and it's important to respect where everyone is at.

We all are and have this beautiful harmonic symphony flowing as part of our essence and so it doesn't matter how it is seen or perceive from the eyes and minds of those that are still under the veils of the 3D world. We must all break free from these old rules and perceptions and feel all the judgment, blame and shame that is still blocking us in a way from fully expressing ourselves in this manner. Deep down it is the energy that matters *not* what it sounds, feels, tastes or looks like because we go beyond what our physical eyes and human senses can perceive. We go down into the depth of it all so that we can feel/sense everything and everyone. The beauty is that more and more of us are finally starting to come out, starting to sing and dance to the rhythm of their own song, their hearts and Souls. We are the first ones that have to give ourselves permission because the old world sure won't do it first. We have to open ourselves, feel it all and see ourselves with a new pair of eyes, our own Universal and Cosmic eyes so we can continuously feel and remember that there is beauty and magic in absolutely everything and that each of us came here with our own unique vibrational imprint that is meant to be shared and seen by the world because it activates others too.

 The way we sing or dance or move is perfect exactly how it comes out when it is expressed through the purity of our being. A lot of the times it is only just for us to see and appreciate it and no one else. Many aspects of ourselves get caught up in sharing it with others and although that is important we must be able to do it for ourselves, see ourselves for who we are and what we are bringing forth. If we do it first for the "external" applause, recognition, attention, appraisal, support then we will continuously become trapped in doing things to please others or to receive something in return that makes us feel loved and wanted.

 Remember that all of this must come from inside first. We all have to give ourselves the applause, recognition, attention, appraisal, support, love, encouragement and upliftment that we need and that we did not fully receive when we were growing up. We must become that ourselves because the "outside" world will never replace our own unique Love.

Start expressing, start singing, start moving and dancing for you, so that you can bring that love and give every aspect of you the attention they still seek, want and need.

This creates a beautiful whole-being, becoming whole with all of our inner/wounded aspects and as this occurs we are able to express from a whole new place inside. At one point you may be guided to start sharing it for others and when you do the energy that you're going to be transmitting will be one that touches hearts, opens minds, reminds people of who they are and awakens the body in powerful ways.

Purification of Expression

A lot of us in the old ways moved and did things without pure intentions, we wanted the attention of others, we wanted sex, we wanted love, we wanted comfort and so much more. The way we express is immensely important and we have to start recognizing the energy behind all that we do. Where are we truly coming from? What distortions are playing out here, sexual, control, etc.? Becoming fully aware of our intentions when we express is going to allow us to deal with those feelings and emotions ourselves so that we don't bring those out in ways that can distort our reality. We all come in with the energy of lack in every way possible and this ties in with love and sexuality. The way we express and move has been quite distorted in ways that it activates and triggers these deeply suppressed energies that we didn't learn how to use.

Sexuality is a vast topic but it felt important to bring it up here as it ties in with our voice and dance very much. The energy of sexuality has been distorted, manipulated in more ways that we can imagine and partly because this energy is part of our Source energy, it is creative force energy, extremely powerful and sacred in many ways. Our lack programs, mentalities and experiences have suppressed and separated us from the sacredness of this energy and we have learned to consciously and unconscious use it to force, control, manipulate a lot of aspects in our world. The more we start to open up and feel all the deeply suppressed emotions and beliefs we have towards this energy the more we are going to start to remember what it is and it will evolve into our pure Souls' expression and desires.

Our human sexuality evolves, we stop using this energy like the old ways and instead it becomes a driving force to create just as it was intended but not from lack but from purity. Our old sexual desires, needs and wants take a whole different form and they support us is reconnecting with ourselves, activating deeper levels of our being. Coming to love ourselves in every way and releasing every energy that was suppressing and distorting our forms of expression is a huge part of us learning how to honor this energy.

We must continue to open up to feeling because there is a lot of a sexual distortion that every single one of us comes with and it's not wrong or bad it just is. We have to fully open ourselves and move past the judgment of all the old societal belief systems so that we can free ourselves from the human ways and start to embrace every part of ourselves for what they've been, what they've done and allow ourselves to come back into this deep space of remembering who we actually are regardless of all of that. Any and every form of expression becomes purified the more we feel into everything fully and allow more Light to come through, recode and release everything at a cellular/DNA level.

We all have a beautiful melody to sing and to dance to. Give yourself permission to open up so you can remember all that you are and free yourself from all that you are not. Bring forth the magic and purity so that your expression becomes a way to share who you truly are and remind others of who they truly are as well.

MOVE/SPEAK/WRITE

Energy moves in so many different ways and amongst them all is speaking and writing. We all lost our voice somewhere along the journey because of all the many experiences and situations that our Soul consciously chose to grow and expand from. Of course when we come down here we completely forget about it all and we get pulled down in a sea of limitations and rules, boxes and cords that keep us boxed in and contracted in many ways. When we start to awaken and dive into our inner world we start to remember many things, amongst many of them is: it's safe to speak up. We may not know truly how at the beginning but that's ok, it's a process, it's a moment by moment experience that teaches and assists you in remembering how.

We might start off by recognizing that in fact we haven't been able to speak up, we haven't been able to stand up for ourselves or even say what we really want to say. All of these deeply suppressed energies are so stuck inside that sometimes we don't even know that we have them. It's not until you start to become more present and really honest with yourself about how you feel and how certain things or people or circumstances make you feel. That could very well be the start of a slew of emotions coming out and that's totally ok and necessary. We want to be able to feel it all fully with the body, we want to be able to feel safe expressing how we feel to ourselves; sometimes we don't need to express it to anyone else but just us. It all starts with being open, honest and truthful with ourselves. Sometimes we may feel like it is necessary and appropriate to share and it is all part of tuning in and really asking what aspect of myself wants to share, is it the version of myself that still wants to be validated, noticed, appreciated or wanted? Is it the version of me that feels lost, alone and angry? And then allow yourself to give that to yourself first. Give yourself the validation, the space, the support, the love because no one can give that to you like your Higher Self version can. You are unique and your Higher Self aspect has everything you need if/when you open up to it.

The ability to express as who we are comes out naturally and effortlessly the more we remove the layers and layers of all the energy that is not who we are, the unspoken feelings, unexpressed emotions, suppressed thoughts and so much more. This is where moving this energy out constantly and consciously as appropriately guided is going to do wonders. All that energy has been stuck, stagnant, blocked by layers and layers of conditioning and so as we start to slowly remove the layers of judgment we start to release it fully. We have to constantly remind ourselves that there is no "good/bad", "right/wrong" when we are in our sacred space, this is the space where your Light holds the field for you to feel and say and write and express anyway that is necessary. Curse words, hate words, ugly words, it doesn't matter here, they are just energy and this energy needs to move, it needs to flow out of you so you're no longer holding it in. The more we keep it in, the more likely it will explode out of us in situations that may bring pain and this will only create more distortion and imbalances/karma in the reality. You want to be able to get this out yourself by yourself, just let the energy flow out and feel it fully in your body so that you're not only releasing it with your mind but with your entire body and being. Let it be a whole body/mind experience and purging.

Writing is another amazing exercise for this. Writing has the ability to open us up and express things that may not come out in words, things that we buried so deep inside that we didn't even know they were in there. The hand/ heart connection is very powerful through writing and it offers so much when we are open and willing to do it.

When I gave myself to dive deep into writing my thoughts, feelings, emotions came out as raw and as real as as crude as they needed to. I realized just how much was stuck in there and it was mind blowing and shocking but so liberating all at the same time. It's like all this time I had all these things and I didn't even were blocking me. I realized that as I let out all of my thoughts I was clearing my mental body so much and that enabled more of my Higher Self guidance to come through more and more and it has been a huge life changing experience to say the least.

Words and Thoughts

There is a lot of energy behind words and so much judgment about good or bad words, positive and negative words and words that shouldn't be said or used. We've labeled absolutely everything and that has kept us living in judgment about pretty much everything. Judgment is heavy, so heavy we sometimes don't even feel it, it's as if we had numbed it so much because of how normal it's become. The more we open ourselves the more we start to feel it and as we start to recognize it as an energy held deep inside, the more we start to feel it fully and the more we start to release and dissolve it from the body.

Remember that duality (good/bad) only exist in the third dimensional realm of consciousness because it functions from such a deep level of separation that it literally labels and separates everything. Energy is just energy, it is neutral, it just is, when we label it or judge it we ourselves create a discordant frequency and we hold that in our bodies which then creates much imbalance in our system. The less we judge things and just see them as energy the freer we become. When we can recognize the energy behind everything we start to see it from a different perspective. Now the funny part is sometimes to release the judgment we have to express how we truly feel as loud as we can no matter what words or thoughts or emotions come up. For instance the 3D world has many purposes but some parts of ourselves may still feel/believe how "terrible, horrible, ugly, bad, evil" it all is perceived to be. Feel into these words, there is still much judgment, duality, anger, pain, grief, and so very much more behind these words. In order to see the world from a different perspective you have to say and feel all that you still hold inside about these old systems.

Everything that is going on in the 3D world is activating an emotion within you so that you can become free of it! Quite fascinating but in many ways what's happening "out there" is simple, it is basically showing/triggering/activating a frequency that you must feel inside of you. It's literally like it's giving you your keys back so you can set yourself free. But if we keep looping in circles in our linear minds about how "ugly and terrible" it is then we are missing the point and not allowing the 3D to support us in the ways that it actually is.

So keep feeling, writing and expressing EVERYTHING in your own sacred space. The more you honor this fully and completely without excuses or shame or guilt your body will do miraculous things. This will open you up to receive more Light and this Light is what recalibrates your whole body so you can be more at peace inside. Inner peace is what creates world peace, when you start to see, recognize and innerstand how absolutely everything is supporting you, us, the whole planet in countless ways without exception you're going to be able to hold peace instead of judgment about all that is transpiring. Plus your reality will drastically shift and merge with the New Earth gridding systems that are already here on this planet. Gaia already holds the New Earth templates and grids in place and now it's up to each and every single one of us to make the necessary space in our bodies to transcend the old and welcome in all the New Earth codes. It is all a process, a magical journey and it is all happening right now; the beauty now is that if you consciously go all in on this ride the experience is so beyond magical and so much more smoother that you actually get to enjoy it and appreciate every bit of it so keep opening up more and more and more and don't ever stop. You're more than ready!

Cry/Scream

There is powerful cleansing and purification sequence that activates when you allow yourself to physically release your emotions. Many of us grew up with the subconscious belief that letting out an emotion through crying or screaming was wrong or bad and many of us were punished for it. Since a very young age we learned that doing this would get us into trouble and so we learned to suppress it to the degree that it became a natural and automatic thing to do. A lot of this journey entails releasing and letting go of the old emotional conditioning that we were taught and accepted as true. There isn't anything wrong with expressing your emotions in a physical way that allows for a deeper clearing and cleansing and so the more we give ourselves permission to release in the ways we are guided in the most appropriate place and manner we will start to feel true freedom.

It's Ok to Cry

Because many of us didn't receive the support or even the permission to physically express an emotion we must now do this for ourselves now. Reminding ourselves, talking to that scared child and letting him or she know that it is now safe to express themselves, it is now safe to feel all that they still have inside; everything that they didn't get to fully feel, everything that they didn't get to express or release about what they thought, what they believed, or how they felt is going to have to come out at some point. What's important to also remember is that the physical release of these energies needs to be in a safe place when it's appropriate. A lot of the times our ego wants the attention, wants the validation and the way that he/she may want to express might come out inappropriately and so it is going to be really important to create a sacred space whether in your home or even outside where you can feel safe and open enough to feel everything fully on your own.

When you allow yourself to be in a place where you can relax, honor, embrace and physically release all the heaviness still stuck inside you will feel your body becoming lighter and freer. The more you come to this space and fully release you will no longer have the need to express your emotions for others to see or validate because you will notice that most of the time the only person that needs to see, hear or validate your own emotions is yourself. Not to say that it's wrong if someone offers you that space but from my experience sometimes when we are on our own space without anyone else's energy we are able to cry harder, yell louder and get all the energy out without anyone else being disturbed or worried about us. There is still much conditioning on every person and so they may not fully innderstand your process and so if you can allow yourself to do the physically release all on your own you'll have much more Mastery of your own clearing process without needing or depending on anyone else to be there with you every time.

Physical Purification

From my experience crying has been a huge purification process that goes deep into the cellular recalibration and reprogramming of your body. A lot of the times my body needs a lot of rest and sleep after I cry and this is important to honor. The more you allow yourself to rest the more your LightBody is able to clear deeper and deeper levels of your body without your linear mind or ego aspects inter-fearing in the process.

Remember that every single organ and cell has to be purified in every way and most of the deep cellular process is achieved through the Light codes that you allow inside of your body. Every heavy emotion is a toxin and it creates more toxicity inside of your body. The more you feel and open up to these heavy emotions the more you will assist your body in cleansing itself from these toxins. These toxins create more of the "normal" toxins that we may be more familiar with that create imbalances in your body and so the less emotional toxins you carry inside the less overall toxins you will have in every organ of your body.

Again, the physical emotional release is crucial for every single one of us to fully honor and allow. Start to consciously let go of the old programming that says crying is weak, crying is for girls, crying makes you more emotional, all of this created a subconscious resistance to crying and it is completely opposite of what crying actually is. Keep releasing yourself from the old 3D belief systems and completely open up to the experience. Create a space where you feel you can let go and feel everything no matter what it is and when you do you will start to feel the power that crying actually creates.

Without Reason

There are moments throughout this phase that you may feel the need to cry without really knowing why or for something that seems so small and insignificant. Let go of what the mind things or perceives because there will be many, many times where your emotions will get triggered and activated and you may not fully know exactly why. This is where letting go of the need to know why or to make sense of it will greatly assist you because you don't need to know why you are crying and you definitely don't need to have a "good" reason to do it either. When your body gets activated and you feel the need to cry, you cry, you feel it all, without questioning it or resisting any of it. Trust that your body is guiding you or may force you at times to let out those tears for a higher purpose. Remember that all of our existences are simultaneously playing out in every moment and so while in this current existence it may not make sense something probably triggered a deep unconscious memory or experience that is still activately playing out in another existence and you just need to honor it and feel it fully.

Anger

There is much of this frequency deeply suppressed inside each and every one of us and it needs to come out. So many events are happening right now that are triggering this more than ever before and it is going to be very important for each of us to feel it fully and honor it. It may come out as frustration, rage and much more and we need to allow ourselves to feel this. Yelling is only one of the many physical ways in which we may be guided to release and so we need to come up with creative ways in which it is safe and appropriate of course. Punching a pillow or yelling at a pillow is a way for us to release some of that anger. Again, I've learned to deal with these emotions on my own without needing anyone there and so open yourself up to finding ways in which you can do this as well.

Underneath the anger we hold inside is a lot of hurt and pain and as we allow ourselves to feel and release the anger you will start to feel all that was underneath it; don't suppress it keep feeling it all and keep feeling it fully with your whole body and being so that you can free yourself from it. There is no shame in having all of these deeply suppressed emotions because trust me we all have them, whether we admit to it, whether we recognize it or whether we believe it, it doesn't really matter because in order to incarnate into this body everyone had to agree to carry a huge load of density.

Continue to open up more and more to all that you feel and continue to honor the physical release that your body will need to engage in to let the energy out. Remember these emotions are just energy and as such they need an outlet in which to let it all out. The less you judge them or judge yourself for having them the easier it will be for your entire body to fully open up and dissolve them.

CREATE

  We were born to create, re-create and rebuild our entire world. The essence of Source/Prime Creator is within all of us, it isn't some being up in the sky separate from us; we aren't far removed from this force and we never have been even though it may physically appear like that but this is only when we chose to incarnate in this plane we seem so separated from absolutely everything. Yes, we all have our own individual form in a body but the energy and essence that makes up who we are is the exact same one that makes up everything.

  We are Source Creator Beings experiencing different aspects of ourselves and in this unconscious world that we created we get to experience coming back into full consciousness, remembering all that we are and all that we've been. The unconscious mind lived under the illusion that fear exists, or that we are separate from one another, that there are other things or beings greater and stronger or even that there are malevolent forces "out there" that can harm us. All of these are projections of the mind that are created through the immense separation held inside of the body. Most everything in the body was disconnected, our DNA was shut down and dormant, our hearts were closed, our muscles were tighten and so there wasn't enough flow and room for things to flow in Unity as it was all intended.

We come here and experience extreme polarity, duality, pain and suffering and at times far greater than our minds/bodies/hearts can bear.

This period on earth is waking us all up, the Light pouring through is shining on all that was hidden and all that was forgotten. We are starting to remember how things truly are and slowly but surely we are coming out of our deep slumber and feeling the pure essence that is inside us all. We start to see the world differently, how we are all connected, how everything has a higher/bigger purpose, how things in our world aren't flowing the way we had hoped and we start to open up to new things, new realities and new perspectives. As we begin to connect with all that's around us and even more so with all that is within us we start to feel the essence of our pure power, our Creator Source power. Our thoughts, our words, our ideas, our emotions, our visions, our goals, our desires all have power within them too. We get to create what our Soul desires, it's not by chance or accident that things happen, our frequency inside is what creates everything.

Our bodies hold the foundation of everything we see "outside", all of our experiences, our relationships, our health, everything we accomplish and gain all stems from our own vibrational response to it.

Old vs. New

Just because we weren't aware or conscious that we were creating every part of our reality doesn't mean it wasn't happening because it's always been happening, we were just so blinded that we had absolutely no clue this was going on. The energy we hold inside becomes a gravitational pull that materializes that same energy/frequency. We become mirrors of all that we see "out there" because everything we perceive to be "outside" is in fact stemming from deep inside of us. At the beginning we have so much stuck and hidden inside that the only way that we can become aware of it is by projecting it "out there" so that it grabs our attention. For many and for a long time, we get stuck on what's "out there" too much, we get fixated, we judge it, we fight it not truly remembering that that is only a reflection of what we need to see within ourselves. It becomes kinda of a cosmic joke when we realize the jokes on us and the answers to all of our problems have literally been under our noses. That often triggers it's own set of emotions which is also part of the process but it is meant to bring a sigh of relief with it, a feeling of freedom, a glimpse of who we are and a call back to all going even deeeeeeeeeeeeeeper inside of ourselves.

When we were asleep and unconscious we created our reality from our own fears, lacks, judgments and deeply suppressed emotions. Somewhere inside we believed or thought that we had to be this person, have this job, get this degree, have this business, achieve this accomplishment because somehow it would fill a lack, a void we felt inside, the loved we never truly received and the support we always wanted and needed. Slowly we start to recognize that doing all of these things doesn't fill the void and sometimes it even amplifies it creating more of an emptiness that keeps us searching for more, wanting more, spending more, working harder and creating more lack and stress in our reality. We didn't learn to value ourselves and see/appreciate ourselves for who we truly are and so everything around us kept feeing the "I am not good enough" story and mentality.

We created so much walls, barriers, boundaries, blocks all around our hearts and bodies that all we ever kept creating was from this deeply wounded, unfulfilled, lack place inside of us and the more we tried to fill it with the outside recognition and material objects the more empty we felt inside. Breathe into all of this and remember that everything you truly need as a Soul is already inside, we already hold the pure love, the peace, the support, the wholeness ,we just forgot. Instead of continuing to focus on the "outside" reality and hoping one day that it will change start to really truly look "inside". Bring yourself to look deeper than you've ever looked before.

A year ago I was guided to rent a hotel room for three days and just stay there on a whole self retreat experience to go deeper inside. I was going through a physically and very deeply emotional phase at the time and during that time at the hotel I started to see deeper parts of myself. At one point I realized that one of the reasons why I would rarely stare at myself in the mirror in a public setting is because I actually did not want to look at myself, I didn't want to confront myself, I didn't want to see all that I still had within myself and at the time my left eye had been completely shut down and so even that was a confirmation of just how much I didn't want to look at myself. It was such a mind blowing, powerful, intense revelation for me at the time that triggered a slew of deep heavy emotions that I allowed myself to feel all three days during myself retreat experience. I literally just slept, cried, ate and bathe all day and all night but yet it was an extremely powerful freeing experience.

There is so much about ourselves that we don't want to see especially when it comes to everything that we have experienced and created that was less than pretty, loving or joyful. We may go through periods of disbelief, rage and grief and it is all part of the process. It is important to feel fully absolutely EVERYTHING for all its glory and all its horribleness.

Let go of the judgment of it all for that will keep you bound to the cords, attachments, contracts and you will keep recreating a physical experience over and over and over until you finally decide to feel everything without judging anything at all. The more you start to feel everything no matter how difficult, challenging and painful it is at times you start to expand into a new thought, a new remembered state in which you start to feel that if you created that experience then that means you can create a different one, you can experience something completely different and new. Yes, as Infinite and powerful Creators we literally have no boundaries, no limits, no blocks, no stories of lack and no fears because the essence of who we are is literally everything and as everything we can create, re-create, collapse, destroy as highest aligned for the good of our Soul's journey and all that exists.

The deeper we go inside the more we start to really feel our pure essence and we start to feel more of what we've created that no longer serves that purity. Our entire realities have to be re-aligned and this is part of the process for each and every single one of us. Taking responsibility for ourselves and our creation becomes an every moment choice and decision because we no longer give our power away. When we were asleep and unconscious we gave our power away to everything, our thoughts, our suppressed emotions, our unhealed aspects, parents, partners, our "outside" world, authority figures, rules and laws and pretty much everything, mostly because we didn't know any better, we didn't know we had the ability to create our reality through our energy. Now more than ever before more and more of us are starting to remember, starting to feel, starting to know, and return back to our Source essence.

It might be a bit scary at first, returning to be full blown creators of our entire reality, or becoming fully responsible for everything and making the necessary choices to recreate our reality to one that is aligned with your Soul. Our ego aspects are very scared and even threatened at the thought of all of this. You see, our ego is the aspect of ourselves that believes so much in the concept of separation that it holds on to the idea that it is small, weak, powerless, fragile, dumb, incapable, disable, fracture and the list goes on; any type of belief or knowing that says the contrary of what it perceives to be true is a literal threat to its existence because it is comfortable being small, blaming others, waiting for others to change first, controlling from lack, telling the same old victim stories because it doesn't actually want to change, it fears change, it fears responsibility, it fears power, it fears its own Light because it doesn't remember anything at all. These are all aspects that rest within each and every single one of us, no one is free from it because we actually need this aspect as separation itself in order to come into this body and so it is what it is. But the important thing is to start becoming more conscious and aware of all of these aspects inside so that we can start to connect back with them. Deep down all they need is your love, your attention, your time, your support and to know that no matter what they've done, what they've gone through, what they feel and think they will still be loved and accepted. Nothing that we've ever done will ever change the pure love that we are and the essence that we hold. At the end of the day it is just an experience, a tool we chose to assist us in returning back to remembering who we are through the continual opening up of our pure hearts.

The more we start to dissolve every single ego aspect we hold inside the more our Light and purity grows inside. We start to remember more and more of our essence as Creators and what we are capable and it all becomes less and less scary and daunting. We start to slowly embrace everything that we are and hold on to our pure power so that we can re-align everything in our reality to reflect who we truly are.

As Source Creator you can create anything, now the tricky part becomes creating things that support your Light in every way possible instead of creating something that continues to feed the ego aspects. Now we move from creating from lack to creating from our pure love, we also move from creating anything to *only* creating that which supports our own Light, Soul journey and also the entire planet. Before when we were functioning from an extreme sense of lack and separation that we were only thinking about ourselves, we only wanted things for us, to feed our ego lack mentalities, we didn't really care about anyone or anything because we were so disconnected and so we actually couldn't feel or see that what we wanted was destroying our Soul and the planet as well.

However things are drastically changing now with all that is transpiring on the planet. We are starting to see more and choose differently, we are starting to really remember that as Creator Beings we came here to create a whole new experience for ourselves and for the whole world, we came here to create only that which supports, amplifies and aligns with who we are as a Soul/Light instead of as an ego.

Continue to feel all that you are and allow all of your Light to come in every way possible because as you do you'll start to remember that you don't need to feed the ego anymore but only your pure Light in every way possible.

Materialize

There is a shift in consciousness that occurs where we start to master the materialization process, not just the manifesting one. Manifesting is the same as creating, the creation process is instant, it is actually done as soon as you think it, imagine it, speak it, write it or intend it because as you do any of this the energy already exists. The fun part is actually opening up so that it becomes a reality in your physical world. Creating and manifesting is super easy at first, it is natural and we are always doing it all the time. Now we have to hold the necessary frequencies, space, systems and gridding structures in place in every part of our body/field/being in order to bring it into our world as a tangible experience.

Now this many take seconds or it may take years, it all depends on what you still hold inside, how much Light you hold, how much ego programming/belief systems are anchored amongst other things. The more you start to feel absolutely everything in every way, in every capacity, you're going to start to open up and receive more information, clarity, guidance, wisdom, knowledge that will support you in making the space and opening up the portals needed to allow that thing to come into your reality.

Portals are so much fun as I'm remembering more and more how they fit into the bigger picture. We open up portals as simply as expanding our own mind, hearts and consciousness. Then our body starts to expands, we expand our hearts, muscles, bones, cells, and this opening becomes the physical portal in which many things come through. When we open up portals we get to shift dimensions, we walk through new realities, open up to gifts and blessings, allow opportunities to come through, we bring back aspects deeper inside and many other things. This opening is literally like opening up a door for things to come in and also for things to leave. Everything that we don't need, that still feeds our lack mentalities, that keeps us scared and contracted is released/dissolved/restored back to Light and therefore creates more space/room for all things that fully supports, uplifts, expands, awakens deeper and deeper parts of our Soul. It is quite fascinating.

We all have an intrinsic gridding system held inside of the body that link up to every code inside and "out", these are constructs that then materialize in your physical world. Some take up more linear time because the constructs inside of your body are not fully built yet and so they require more from you. This is when full and complete consciousness is requires so that you can stay open to the signs, messages, guidance steps needed in order to build the support system that will make that appear in your reality. Yes, much patience, surrendering and allowing yourself to go with the flow of things is much required for the more you do this the easier and faster these grids will build inside of your body.

On the other hand, there are support systems that are already in place inside that as soon as you ask for something everything lines up and it is delivered at the foot of your doorstep (literally!), it is way cool. And yet you have been building and reconstructing these systems for a while now, long before you even had that specific idea/need/want pop into your head. It is as if you already knew that the time will come in which you would be fully and totally ready and once the idea popped into your head everything was already fully aligned and ready for you to receive it.

This is just part of how we each encoded our reality. Some things will take "longer" based on the belief systems we have towards that thing and some things will be a lot easier to materialize and all will be perfect. Each will be part of an experience that you encoded yourself with to allow you to keep going, have more trust, have more focus, open up more and feel the support you need in that moment.

The more you continuously open up you'll get to a point where you have such deep trust, deep awareness, keep knowing that everything is perfectly aligning as it should. There is no need to push, force, pull in the way we used to do it in the old days because this creates more karmic timelines and instead if we just fully open up and surrender to our Soul as it guides us, directs us, reconnects us and creates magical opportunities that will support us in materializing all that we need and want then it will be so much more fun, joyous, blissful, magical and magnificent in every way. Time completely dissolves and so we don't look at the time anymore to see if it has arrived, or ask ourselves why it's not here yet, we don't allow anything in our experience to be a sign of lack or us not being good enough because we fully innerstand just how this all works and if we keep focusing and listening and trusting and opening up all will "fall" in place in the most perfect timing.

It truly does become quite simple and fun as you continue to ascend higher and higher in frequency. We don't struggle, or work hard or hustle like we thought we needed to back in the old days, we just go with the flow, we surrender, we embrace, we sing, we dance, we enjoy every moment and every second as that is part of the entire process and we just continue to shine as Bright as possible and hold the frequencies needed in place. It truly becomes a simple, magical and beautiful experience that we actually get to enjoy and play with the more we are open to it.

BUILD

This is all about building and rebuilding a whole new society that functions from the purity of their love, joy and peace. This linear year of 2022 is a massively important moment in our planet's history because it is ushering an incredibly huge amount of builder frequencies also knows as Master Builder codes and Source codes. This is one of the many imprints that the number 2 brings with it. There will continue to be a massive collapse, dismantling and destruction of what we refer as the old third dimensional realm of consciousness to herald a completely new one deemed as the New Earth or Heaven. For many sometimes this term is confusion as the way we pictured or had been taught about Heaven differs from the way we speak of it now. Heaven and Hell have always been on this planet but the old 3D systems and structures created the idea that these places were only experienced after you transitioned out of this human form instilling much fear and control. And so for a long time we felt that we had to subdue to their ways of existing because we believed that *that* was the only way to reach Heaven and not be condemned to Hell.

Again, we have been living in Heaven and hell on this planet all this time without even being conscious of it. The 3D realms of consciousness are actually hell, it is where we are dormant, completely asleep, following "external" rules and norms and living surrounded by much fear and lack. As one starts to wake up and discover that there is more to everything we have been told and taught, we start to become more open to that which seemed unreal and untrue like energy, spirits, the quantum realms, and so much more. We start to dive into the world of spirituality which is the 4th Dimensional realm of consciousness. This is where we start to see the ugliness and distortions of the 3D world and we go deep into our emotions to clear the separation that was deeply embedded in our cells and DNA. In this realm is where we start to become more conscious and responsible of our roles. We start to remove things in our reality so that we can be open to new things, new opportunities, new relationships, new jobs, new careers, new locations that are more in alignment with who we are, what our passions are and what actually fulfills our Souls.

The process of fully transitioning out of the lower realms of 3D and 4D is an individual journey for all and the timeframe that it takes is very personal as well. It all depends on how invested, focused, commitment and willing you are to going deeper than you've ever gone before, feel more than you've ever felt before, remember more than you ever have or thought you could. Our inner path, Soul journey and ascension passageway become priority and we start to let go of so many things, relationships, jobs, careers, identities, objects, beliefs, and so much more.

In reality we are always building, we are always creating but now we must be fully conscious of what we have built and created that wasn't pure, that was only feeding fear and lack, and then we have to consciously rebuild and re-create it from scratch.

When we get to fully ascend our consciousness into the 5th Dimensional realms, we reach zero point more fully with our whole being and from this point everything must be rebuilt. It might seem daunting, overwhelming and frustrating from a lower perspective but trust me when you reach this point and ascend you will be completely at peace with it all and exciting that you're finally going to be creating from a much more conscious, Soul-aligned, pure based space inside that will support you in so many beautiful ways.

Physical Rebuilding

Our whole world and planet is undergoing a massive rebuilding process but it's important to remember that in order to fully assist in this process each and every single one of us must be willing to rebuild their own physical structures, energetic foundations and tangible reality. It all starts with us truly, and the more we do it within ourselves the easier it will be to then apply that to rebuilding our world.

In the 4D level of consciousness we feel a need to go out there and rebuild the world but yet we still have a lot of emotional baggage we are carrying and so a lot of our emotions come out. This is essentially where most of the collective is, it is in a space where things are becoming so unbearable, unjust, controlled that they are fighting, they are showing their anger and frustration in hopes that this changes things but in reality the long lasting and huge changes that we wish to create in the world must start with our own personal and inner changes. So even though that has a huge role and purpose for many to start seeing just how distorted things are in the 3D world, we get to a point that the fighting and the pushing and the resistance we have towards the system only creates more of that.

When we are able to consciously step away and go deeper within ourselves, go all in with our emotions, resolve and integrate our most wounded aspects, recognize our belief systems and what is truly going on inside of ourselves then and only then can lasting change occur. The systems of the old world are inside, we are the ones holding them in our bodies, we are the ones that created them and supported them unconsciously and the more we become conscious of this and conscious of who we are and the pure power we hold inside the smarter we become about rebuilding our world.

It's not the easiest path to go; I will tell you that now. In fact some of us avoided going inside for a long time, we didn't want to travel that far in, we didn't want to know what we still had inside, we didn't want to feel all over again the hurt, pain and trauma, and so we kept hiding from it, avoiding it, suppressing it further and further in until we reach a point where we no longer can; our bodies are literally screaming now so that we can no longer run away from our baggage and fully feel it to release it.

Every part of our body is waking up now, the Light that is entering the planet, our fields and our bodies are shining on every aspect of ourselves that is heavy, distorted, separated and occult. We are coming to that point where we don't have a choice, the separation, the control, the suffering that we are continuing to create in 3D hell is unbearable, too much to handle, and it is creating more and more chaos, destruction, battle and much more. This of course serves a purpose in waking up more and more people and even more within ourselves. But we start to realize that there is a better way and that we are ready to live different and so instead of waiting for that "out there" to change we start to change ourselves. We must, there is literally no other way, for the only way that our world can change is by becoming that same change we wish to see out there.

It all starts inside. Looking at what we are still holding inside, what we are still fearing, what we believe about ourselves, our "past", our choices, our everything. And then start to open up in every way. Everything we have in our physical reality represents something we are holding on to inside; it equates to a system, either a fear-lack based system or a pure-love based system. And when we are able to recognize which system each aspect of our reality supports then we are able to consciously decide to remove it, replace and rebuild it in every way that we are Soul-guided.

The rebuilding process is literally an every moment experience because as we open up our hearts, we start to become more aware, more present, more in-tuned with everything that is around us and as this occurs we start to feel what needs to go and what can stay. Every aspect of our reality has to be re-evaluated, we have to constantly check what everything in our reality is feeding: is it feeding me more joy or more lack, is it creating more peace or more stress, is it in alignment with my Soul or an ego aspect of myself; yes we start to really look at everything and scrutinize it with a Cosmic eye (instead of judgmental one). Everything is just an energy and so when we can feel the energy behind everything we have, everything we say, think and everything that comes into our reality, we are able to determine what role it plays, what aspect of myself is it feeding, and if it has any attachment to the old version of myself. As we become more and more aware we then consciously release/remove it as appropriate it.

Purity of INtent

This journey becomes about consciously building and rebuilding everything and so we must constantly check our intentions. Are we building this to receive something in return that we still feel we lack inside? Are we building in a way that is highest aligned, that supports my Light, honors Gaia and all beings? Or are we building from an aspect that still feels unloved, unsupported and unrecognized? And just feel everything that comes with these questions. You're not bad or wrong or unworthy if you recognize that yeah, somewhere inside I was wanting to build this or start this thing because of the money, or success that I can have. There isn't anything wrong with owning that and I've had to do that plenty of times. Just being ok with owning how you feel and where you are really coming from in every aspect of your life is monumental, especially because we have an unconscious and automatic tendency to not admit it or not look at that aspect of ourselves because it would bring shame or guilt... trust me we all have these aspects and these emotions. It's not wrong to feel this, it isn't wrong to have these aspects it's just not truly who we are at our core and it creates more suffering inside when we don't fully own them.

At the very core of it all it is only an emotion or belief that is tied to an aspect that is holding on to an experience that still hasn't been fully resolved, dissolved and integrated inside. That's it. And again we ALL have these emotional aspects but it's just that we haven't fully learned to deal with this and we held on to the idea of what was "right/wrong, good/bad" which separated us even more from them.

Give yourself permission to open up fully, let go of what you once thought was true, let go of the old belief systems even just a little bit and open up to just connecting with everything that you are, everything still stuck inside that just wants your time, space, attention and love, sometimes it just wants you to look at these aspects and recognize what they are still holding on to so that you can create the space they need so they can feel, release, let go and come back inside. Don't judge any of it, don't judge yourself or any version of yourself, just be with it, hold the space it needs and you'll stat to see the beauty that comes from it, the love that emerges from just you honoring this aspect and embracing it back into your love...nothing can compare to this and it is the key to everything.

The Divine Child

The integration of your wounded aspects births your Divine Child. This is one of the many Higher Self aspects that we are and it becomes more and more present the more and more we unify with more separated aspects. This is a huge part of the process because as this occurs we get to build in a whole new way as well. We get to bring the aspects of pure fun, play, simplicity, innocence, love, acceptance and so much more. The building and rebuilding process becomes a pure joyous experience that we unify with, it becomes who we are because we are builders at our core. We are no longer building from lack, rushing and pushing, hustling and bustling, pushing against the flow, we instead become one with the Divine Flow of all and we get to enjoy every moment of this rebuilding process.

The ease and grace that comes through as we flow and play and embrace is indescribable at times. There is such peace, such effortlessness at times, everything just comes and we get to open up to the magic and beauty of being fully present in every way.

Continue to open yourself to this process and the more you do the more you'll start to remember how worthy it all becomes.

FLIP

There is a flipping and reversal of everything as you ascend and fully anchor into the heavenly realms. The old world was backwards and inside out in every way and so absolutely everything has to be returned and restored so that it can be in full alignment with your Soul/Light. It is an every moment process and constant observation of everything inside and around so that you can start to tell where things are coming from, where is the root of it all, is it coming from fear/lack or pure Love/Light, is it feeding an ego based construct/mentality or is it nourishing your Light/LightBody? Becoming open and aware is truly the most important step because the more that you do this in every moment the more answers will come through.

The Reversal Process

This reversal process goes very deep, down to the core of your cells and DNA. Everything actually was literally backwards, it spun backwards creating a resistance and tightness in the flow of how all should operate and it's also why the 3D consciousness world was so harsh, hard, painful and distorted; nothing ever "worked", nothing fit our Soul, nothing fulfilled us fully, and it was never meant to because of the mechanics of how everything functioned at an energetic level.

It is only when you start to disconnect from it all, separate and start going deeper inside, reconnecting with your body, heart, Soul, essence that you start to see/feel the misfit of it all. That's when you start to realize and remember that the reason why you felt like you didn't fit in, like you were an outsider, a black sheep, an outcast, a rebel, a crazy fool, and just so much more is because at an energetic level nothing felt "right or true". It was so out of alignment with who we were and we could feel it, we could sense and therefore we chose to see things differently or do things differently while not knowing exactly why. Something deep down inside just felt like the old "outside" world did not make sense. Some of us at some points in our lives did go against it and at some times we were drawn back into it, and it is all part of the journey that we all chose to experience. They were things that I didn't want and didn't do and yet others that I went ahead and followed the system. All in all, it taught and activated a great deal of things within me and I am grateful for it all and the more I continue to expand and remember the more I see the purposes of those experiences.

When we start to listen to and follow our hearts, Soul, body more and more and more we start to put a halt to the old systems and structures inside. The more and more we continue to go against our ego wants, needs and desires the more we start to become guided by our pure essence. Of course, this is no easy task because as this occurs our ego starts to resist, fight and feel more of what it had suppressed. This is where the emotional journey comes in play, all of the deeply unconscious suppressed emotional energies start to get activated so that you can feel and release them fully from the body. This is the energy that our ego/separated aspects have held on to for dear life because they operate under the perception that all of these emotions, stories, experiences keep them safe and protected, they are so emotionally scared of all that it can't see or understand that the only thing it knows is to hold on to everything. As we start to feel all of the emotions that start coming up for us we start releasing an enormous amount of weight, we literally feel like a ton of weight gets lifted off of our shoulders and every other part of our body...our hearts start to open up, we start to feel more relaxed and our bodies start to feel more at peace.

The process that follows is what we refer to as zero point, we reach zero point field after a huge amount of clearing and releasing on a deep cellular level. This is the big stop, the big void, the big pause that we go through and when the necessary space/time has gone by everything starts to reverse itself and things flip. Our bodies do this for us, they know the natural flow of things and so they start to move in the direction that all must go in order for everything to be fully balanced. This is also part of your Merkaba activating. .

The Merkaba

Our Merkaba is part of what we refer to as our energy field or auric field. It is formed by two inverted tetrahedron pyramids that constantly rotate. The one pointed upwards represents the masculine energies and the one pointed downwards represents the feminine energies. When we live in the old unconscious realities of the 3rd and 4th dimensional realms these two pyramids spin in reverse, they are literally going the natural and organic flow of energy and it is again why things in these realms are hard and harsh, we try, we work hard, we push and pull trying to play in the resistance game but with no avail as we are going against our own natural and organic flow.

These two opposite energetic forces have to completely recalibrate in order to regain their normal directional spin. Again it is a process, it is not an overnight thing and it is not a mental process either. The mind gets caught in wanting to control, wanting to force, wanting to push this process but it isn't quite like that. It is when we allow the mind/ego to fully surrender to the process and let our Light/LightBody direct and lead and recalibrate that we start to feel this shift. It can start in small increments, we may feel our merkaba start to activate and come online more as gravity goes and then we have to keep opening up and surrendering so that it never reverses again.

With the activation of the Merkaba, our magnetic poles shifts as well, yes our world may seem like it gets flipped over and turned upside down and indeed that is a big part of the process too. Everything we ever worked for, fought for, believed in completely shifts and changes and it no longer has the same value that it once did. Our whole belief system flips, what we thought was once true it isn't and what we thought was false isn't. This is all part of returning to live as Souls instead of living as a separated aspect of ourselves. We shift from operating from our closed linear minds to our open higher hearts and minds. We go from admiring and idolizing the fame and fortune of the old and start to remember what actually matters. The material gains and obsessions completely dissolve and we start to look at it all from a completely different and opposite perspective.

It's important to also remember that this phase of seeing things more clearer and veil thinning will bring many emotions. Anger, sadness, grief, frustration are all so very normal to feel because it literally feels like our whole world falls apart and it is so important to allow yourself to feel it all fully. Don't hold back, don't suppress, don't pretend or fake it for you will only be suppressing it more. This is where being fully open and honest with yourself about it all is going to assist you way more than you can comprehend with your mind but just trust. Your heart will start to feel it and it will start to open up more and more and more to where you'll start the re-alignment of everything. Yes, the ego will have its moments of tantrums and resistance and we all go through them but the more you allow this energy to be felt and released the less you'll be carrying it around with you. We've been holding on to it for soooo long that a lot of the times we didn't even know we had these deep heavy feelings and emotions. Many times you won't what you have inside until you continuously open up and start to feel the deep ugly, heavy stuff and the more you do the freer you become.

Ascension of Consciousness

After you ascend your consciousness you start to become even more aware of how it all works. You start to listen more to your Higher Self and the more you follow it the more you'll continue to fully reverse every single cell in your body. My teacher Lisa said it so well once, if you want to activate your Merkaba, do everything opposite of what your ego wants, and it took me awhile to fully comprehend but I am innerstanding this more and more as I go through my own physical body ascension process.

Your Higher Self aspects will push you and guide you to things that your ego may still be scared of and that is the point. You want to essentially break through all of your fears, ego mentalities, lack constructs because this is what our old realities were based on and so in order to break free we have to break through each and every single one of them so that we can start to exist from the essence of purity, peace, wholeness and joy.

This is where we start to really challenge ourselves to no longer function from the old ways, not give in to the perceived fears or the illusion of lack because if we do we fall unconscious again. When we do we have to reverse everything that we created from this state and bring it back to full consciousness and it may just be way too much energy that we had anticipated. This is why becoming very observant and present in each moment will allow us to see where we are coming from and what aspect of us is coming through. It is also why we go from moving really fast, to slowing everything down, this is so we can start to really feel, sense, see, hear, everything that is going on so that we can then move as a Higher Self and not react or respond from a wounded aspect or suppressed emotion.

Old distortions

When our energy fields and centers spun backwards, our Merkaba spun backwards too. This created ripples of distortions in every way. We functioned from our distorted or unconscious masculine, feminine and child and so all of these energies have to flip and revert so that we can function as our Divine Masculine, Feminine and Chid aspects. All of these energies are held inside of us, we are already whole and complete. This isn't about finding our Divine Masculine or Feminine counterpart to balance us out, instead we must first balance everything we already have inside of us so we can become fully whole in this body again. Yes, we each choose a female or male form but we all have both frequencies inside.

This journey is about returning to this space of wholeness where we activate and become both of these Divine aspects and we can bring whichever is highest aligned in every moment. Eventually as we merge and become everything we become in a way androgynous and we associate with both but not from an egoic or distorted way but from a pure way. All evolves and so we must be open to everything that this process entails, you don't need to fully comprehend, or believe or agree you just have to be open to it because when you are you'll start to remember more and you'll become more conscious of all that is transpiring.

FLY/FLOAT

We are earth angels, avians, that can fly and soar, we are these frequencies and just because we haven' been trained to see/fee/believe that this all exists within us it doesn't mean that it doesn't. Remember that coming down here into the physical body suppressed a lot of our knowing and remembrance because of the level of density that we chose to hold, as of right now there isn't any other way to come down and so at a Soul level we know this. When we start to open up and feel energy, reconnect with that which is not tangible or even believable at times, we start to open up more to all that is held deep inside of us. The magic, the beauty, the surreal becomes more real because we can feel it and at the beginning that is all we need, that is enough to open us up into a new world, a new experience that continues to open us, activate us and remind us of all that is pure and real.

When we come down as kids a lot of our inner knowing stays and we can remember a lot but as we grow up and we get fitted and molded into the 3D societal norms we start to push it all away, suppress it and at some level not believe in it anymore.

This whole entire journey is about remembering everything that we forgot. Sometimes it might seem a bit challenging because a lot of the things literally go against what we've been told, against the narrative, against our family and friends, and it's all normal. It's part of breaking free from the old illusions, the old ways, the old beliefs and the old perceptions. It may not make a lot of linear sense but it will start to make sense in your heart and that is all that matters at the beginning. The mind is used to play tricks on us, we programmed it this way, it's like we created our own video game, with all of the old distorted rules, with all the challenges, villains and levels to surpass so that we can see all that we are capable and just how powerful we truly are. We are rooting for ourselves every step of the way because we know deep down we can do anything, deep down we know that if we created the game, we can get out of it and recreate the entire thing. Obviously it's all a process with many phases and experiences all along the way but if we continue to open up to them we'll start to remember it all.

Angels

The energy of angels, guardian angels, archangels are frequencies that we start to reconnect and activate within ourselves as we open up and submerge ourselves to our journey. At first we start to see/perceive them "out there", and it is all a part of the process but as we start to remember more we start to realize that they are showing themselves as an aspect that we hold inside and it is then when we become angels again. In fact we become everything, we start to open up our wings, we start to feel them, sense them, see them with our inner eyes/vision and we start to remember how to utilize them all over again.

Flying and floating is just one of our natural abilities that we all have. We are meant to fly and be free and not be stuck in the lower realms where we feel stuck, glued to the ground, not able to move or jump. This is all part of how we programmed the 3D realms to be but as we start to see and remember more we start to break free from the chains, the cords, the barriers and the blocks that tie us all back down into hell. The heaviness and density of our bodies kept us in the lower realms, it kept us going in loop cycles, recreating the same painful hardships and experiences and it isn't until we start to release ourselves and clear/cleanse/dissolve all the density stuck inside that we start to experience the lightness of this existence.

Body Density

As the density goes, so does gravity and it is why the body feels very light, floaty, like it's in a higher altitude. Experiences like light headedness, the 3D label vertigo, dizziness, ungroundedness, are part of the physical changes and experiences that one has as you start to release a lot of density and hold more Light. Your Light is weightless, it isn't bound or anchored to the physical dimensions and as so it because freer, it flys, floats, soars and swims in the infinite field of consciousness that is expansive and outside of the linear concepts. Another hugely important thing to remember about these physical experiences is that it will challenge your control and protection mechanisms. When we feel so elevated and floaty we feel like we can't control things, like we have nothing to hold on to that makes us feel secure, like we have to go back down because it isn't safe to fly or be so expanded and so your linear/ego mind will get triggered and it is normal when this occurs. The important thing to remember is to feel whatever comes through and remind yourself that you are ready, you don't need to control anything, you don't need to come back down to hell, you don't need to weight yourself and "ground" yourself in a way that locks you back down to a lower level of consciousness. Allow yourself to be free and fly and feel the density go. If you can be in a space/place where you can fully and completely surrender, sit or lay down, close your eyes or whatever else you are guided to do, do it so that you don't try or control the experience. The more you surrender and just go with the flow and stay as expanded as you can the more you'll adjust to it and the more you'll be able to remember that it is all part of the process.

Contraction

As you allow yourself to fly and float in the higher realms, there is phase when you come back down called the contraction phase where you drop back down to the physical realms and shift everything in your reality that is no longer supported you. In essence you have to see/feel everything that is currently in your reality that needs to be cleared/removed/dissolved so that your whole body can achieve that frequency. When you fly and float at the beginning it is mainly from an energetic stand point, our field and mind expands while we are still in the body. As we contract back down into the body we have to clear everything that is in the body so that we can hold/sustain/anchor the vibrational frequency in order to achieve that energetic altitude and expansion within our entire body.

This is where physical body ascension comes to play. After we continuously expand and ascend in consciousness now we have to bring our entire body with us. Yes, our body has to be able to hold and sustain the Light of our Soul fully and for that to occur we have to create an enormous about of space by clearing the heaviness, the emotions, the toxicity, the old 3d systems and programs and everything else that comes with all of that. It is an every moment process and experience where we open up and we get to observe more of what is in the way and what is truly assisting us, what do we need to remove and add to our reality that will support us, where do we need to go deeper and feel more and relax more so that our bodies can completely open up to receive and anchor more Light.

Other Existences

As we open up more we are going to start to remember more of those other existences still actively playing out in our reality that are showing us where we continuously play small, where we have suppressed our wings, where are we not allowing ourselves to open our hearts and so much more. Because of where our wings are located, behind our hearts/shoulder blade region, the continual opening up and dissolving of all of our hearts, walls, blocks, chains, barriers is going to be a huge aspect of this journey. There are many existences where we literally were killed, persecuted, tortured for utilizing our gifts and abilities or even for believing something other than what was believed at the time and so all of us come in with a huge amount of fear programming that is so deeply unconscious that we don't even know that we have. We have suppressed so much behind our hearts and bodies because we didn't want to deal, feel, or own the heavy stuff. We believed that we were safe hiding behind it and all we were really doing is incarcerating ourselves to realities that we hated and despised.

This takes constant participation and commitment so that we can constantly remind all aspects of our being of what is true and pure so that they can continue to feel safe and tart to open up and release, whether you say it in your mind, out loud, internally feel it with your body, visualizing it in your head and any other way that you are being shown and guided will greatly support. We need to revert the program that says holding on to the old keeps me safe and secure to one that says opening up to release the old ways supports me and allows me to feel more loved. Yes, we begin to consciously reprogram ourselves in ways that serves and supports us in every way so that we no longer exist from the old ways and systems. It takes conscious awareness but the more you do it the easier and easier it becomes.

CLEAN

    The clearing process is very similar to cleaning your house and I mean deep cleaning. Every cell must be cleared and cleansed from the frequencies that disrupt the normal and natural state of each single cell. This is one of the reasons why it is just a complex process that takes linear years and it will just continue to evolve. Everything inside of our bodies need to be cleaned, detoxified and purified at a deep cellular and DNA level from everything that we ever ingested, inhaled, allowed that was of a lower/slower frequency. As this continuously occurs inside we must also take command and start cleaning everything that is part of every level of our reality.

    We clean our bodies by tuning in and asking each organ how it needs to be cleansed. This is a very important step because the mind can get caught up with listening to others peoples advice or suggestions without tuning in inside. Even though we know that everything must be cleared and cleansed it doesn't mean that we need to do it all at once or through the methods that others say. The body is very intelligent and it holds consciousness so when you start to communicate and truly listen and observe/sense what it is trying to tell you you'll start to honor what it needs. Everything from the supplements, foods, liquids to the dosages of each will come through from the body. This is also how we start to regain trust in it as well, instead of trusting the "exterior" world on how one should treat the body. We stop listening to any part of the outside world, stop reading labels and we continuously listen and trust and the more we do the more we get to support ourselves and our LightBody and easier and faster the process will unfold.

Your Space

Everything around you is part of your field, sometimes we get caught up in the numbers and old perceptions but in reality the more you open up, the more your energy field expands and so everything that surrounds you becomes part of what's in your field. This allows us to connect with things more and feel the resonance or the dissonance of all that is around you. We start to take command and make the necessary choices to re-align, reorganize and clean up anything and everything that is causing havoc, stress and an imbalance.

Remember that the "outside" world is a reflection of your inner world and therefore the more you observe it, feel it, open up to it the more you will start to recognize what is still actively playing out inside. This is a simultaneous process, we observe the "outside", while continuing to go deeper inside to feel/clear and then shift our physical reality so that it assist in the recalibration of the entire body/field.

The cleaner, more organized, more spacious, more pure your physical environment becomes the more your body will be and feel supported in this process because every little thing counts. We start to become very observant about our environment and we start to honor it more by cleaning it more, organizing as we are guided, changing things, moving things, relocating things, it becomes a necessary flow that we must constantly adjust to because we innerstand the importance that it makes in every level of our reality. At first it might be misunderstood as some sort of disorder but in reality it is what we need to do to bring things back in order, restore the balance and align with the Divine flow

In the old days, we didn't understand or remember just how everything that surrounds us is really important. Everything plays a huge role in what we are able to create, what keeps us stuck in the old, what keeps us recreating old patterns, what keeps us stressed and fearful, just so much. I've personally started to become so much more aware of how important it is to constantly upkeep my reality, keeping it clean, organized, keep checking up on it even if I have to rearrange and reorganize constantly, at the core of it all it is energy and it is always moving so we don't need to be afraid of doing too much because there is no such thing as long as you are constantly tuning in and listening to your guidance. This is where we have to let go and break free from the old mindsets and perceptions and the "what are others going to think" because this is your reality not theirs, we each have to be fully responsible and accountable about our reality because that is how we become fully responsible about recreating a brand new one that is fully Soul aligned and supportive of New Earth.

This becomes a new flow, a new way of existing, a new dance in which we are totally in sync and connected in every way where we aren't afraid of the choices that we may need to take to realign everything. Open up to everything and you'll start to see the magic that unfolds the more that you do.

STAND UP

    We all have to acquire enough energy/"balls" to stand up for what we know to be true, yes it takes much courage and boldness to do it as we will need to go against the old in many ways. When we start to open up and remember that there is more going on in the world and we start to recognize how the old ways aren't working anymore we have to be able to not allow ourselves to be swayed or pushed back into the old. In many ways, if we do choose that scenario remember that anyone playing a role in your reality is only playing an aspect of yourself that you still need to see/own/feel/connect to. We do choose certain people in our reality that are there to challenge us, activate/trigger something inside so that we no longer go small, go weak or hide. I've had many times where this has happened with my own human family and each time I get to speak a little more, stand up a little more and become braver about doing it too.

    In the early days an emotion would come through and it would get the better of me but as I continue to open up and feel all those things on my own I am able to speak and communicate from a much more stable and calm space inside. A lot of the times I realize that I am also playing a role in activating them in ways that they may not fully comprehend but just by being in each other's fields, space or consciousness we are able to transmit codes at an energetic level that if the other person is ready and open they will receive their own personal activation. It is quite fascinating how all of this works when you start to see and remember more of what it all entails and why you chose certain people in your reality… but back to standing up, yes, this is a constant standing up for your Light, your body, your inner knowing regardless if people will innerstand or not. A lot of the time they don't but because I've achieved a high level of respect towards myself and Soul when I interact with someone that may not fully innerstand I get the aspect of them that still respects me and honors my journey. The more you honor, respect and love every aspect of yourself the more your interactions with other people change and you'll start to receive the same level of honor, respect and love from them. You have to activate that within yourself so that you can activate that in others.

Standing up for ourselves when most of us didn't receive this when growing up is definitely something to grow into but the more you continue to anchor your Light, open up all of your energy centers the more you'll start to speak, share and express in ways that you never did before. I was an extremely shy and introverted kid growing up so it has taken much to be able to grow out of my shell and start to gain the confidence and the courage to speak. Now I am learning and remembering how to speak up as it's appropriate from my deep inner knowing and wisdom and remembrance even when it may not conform with others beliefs or to what's going on in the world.

We have to constantly remind ourselves that we are the rule breakers, the uncomformists, the change makers, the Trail Blazers, the WayShowers and so much more. We didn't come here to play small and play by the old rules but rather exit the old game and create a world where we live in Unity and peace consciousness. A lot of people right now are standing up in ways that they never have before, they are being seen, being bold and courageous and this is part of the process. We all must be open to all of this and how is going to be up to each individual to figure out for themselves. There are aspects of ourselves that are doing it out of anger, frustration, grief and so many other emotions and we have to recognize when our motives and intentions are being fueled by an unresolved emotion. There are many emotions that will continuously be triggered and activated in so many ways and it is important because it is activating those collectives that are still deeply asleep and unconscious. However for many of us that are more aware of what is going on it is going to be important for us to deal with our emotions ourselves, feeling more, releasing more, opening our hearts more so that we can stop fighting the old battles and instead stand up in softer and way more powerful ways than before.

We now have to stand up energetically, physically, emotionally and mentally in our own personal realities by not feeding the old agendas, by not supporting the old ways, by not focusing on the old world in ways that keeps us distracted from what is truly going on inside. If we take what's going on "outside" and utilize it in ways that support our journey in going deeper and deeper and deeper this will be a much more powerful approach that will allow us to start focusing on what really matters: our Soul, our LightBody, our New Earth reality.

We become so much stronger, powerful, bolder when we choose to not play in the old game anymore and rather play in the New, play as Light, play in the rebuilding and reconstructing of our own internal and physical realities in ways that obliterate the old much faster than we thought possible.

This is about exercising the pure power that we hold as Light, standing up as Light, becoming the peace and unity that we are and no longer entertaining the old. If you open up yourself to a much softer but yet way more powerful way of dismantling the old while reconstructing the New you'll start to see that there is no need to fight or battle the old anymore. All we have to do is keep standing strong in our Light, holding our Light, expanding our Light and not dimming it ever again. This will create ripples of change in the most powerful and groundbreaking ways, you just have to keep opening up and fully trusting in the inner process.

SLEEP

Where do I start with sleep. This is another huge part of the process that sometimes precedes all. If you can allow yourself to honor the phases where all you do is sleep, it will be extremely powerful. Yes, I was being extremely serious, there will be phases where your body will knock you down and over the head and you will not be able to function in any capacity and so all we can do is fully surrender to sleeping. This is one of those practices that actually become more important than even meditation. This is where you are able to fully surrender, unwind, shut off the monkey mind and allow your LightBody to restore, repair, clear tons of density, recalibrate and anchor without your conscious participation. When you fully honor this process and phase you will be supporting your LightBody and this process in ways that may not make sense but in more ways than you would if you were consciously participating.

Your linear/ego mind is still operating under deep levels of separation so it doesn't fully innerstand what is going on and it will start injecting fear, it will try to label things, it will try to fix or think something is wrong, it will try to stop or inter-fear with the whole thing because it is going against what 3D doctors say. This is just an extremely normal part of the process, in fact the whole physical body ascension process actually goes against everything we were taught and is still believed from a 3D level of consciousness because the whole 3D realm was backward and polar opposite of how things actually are. Are you feeling me now?

The more you allow yourself to fully surrender to this process in every way, the more you'll support your LightBody in all the upgrades and repairs that it is trying to do to assist you in achieving/anchoring the 5D Heavenly realms inside of your body. Everything is created from what you hold inside of your body at a deep cellular and DNA level and so the more you allow your Light to repair and rebalance it the more your body will be able to increase its Light quotient in a way that allows you to experience a New Earth reality.

The Old Ways

In the old days we were taught that we had to sleep a certain amount of hours at specific hours of the day, everything was rules and structures and programming that actually went against our own body's rhythm. There might be "facts" and results out there but remember everything was mostly done under a 3D level of consciousness and most of us are not taught how to listen to our own body and its needs. Everyone is different; every LightBody goes through different phases and so now that more and more people are being activated in so many different levels and ways our old ways of functioning in this life are drastically changing.

You may go through phases where all you do is sleep in order to clear an enormous amount of density, anchor a large amount of photonic Light and rebalance your entire body systems. There may be phases where you integrate so much Light that you may have little to no sleep. And other phases your sleeping and waking states actually flip and merge. Your night becomes day and your day becomes night. This all happens at different phases and during different processes for each and every single one of us and so if you allow yourself to let go and release all of the previous facts and 3D information you had about your body and just start to listen to your LightBody it will be extremely supportive in every level.

When you are being called to sleep during the day and be awake all or most of the night, it's normal, this is part of the reversal process that your body goes through. As previously mentioned EVERYTHING has to be reverted, flipped and reversed and so flipping your sleep cycles supports with this. Another thing that is also occurring here is you start to anchor the dream state; yes, we start to live in a dreamy world, a dreamy reality where all our pure dreams and desires start to anchor and materialize in our reality. Everything becomes dreamy and fuzzy at times because it all moves and bends and breathes. Nothing is ever fixed anymore, in fact in never truly was we just believed that it was and held so tight to that belief that we created an internal structures in which realities were very solid, firm and too rigid to mold in a way that supported us. All of this starts to dissolve and dissipate the less and less we hold those fixed, rigid structures inside of our physical bodies and we start to open up more.

Realities are meant to breathe, move and shift in a Divine flow that supports us. As we continue to anchor more of the 5D New Earth frequencies inside we start to feel this more and more in our core. We start to feel the density and heaviness of our old 3D realities and how fear, stress, lack creates such an imbalance inside of the body. The more we release ourselves from these frequencies the more we open up and remember that our lives aren't supposed to be this heavy. We are meant to be free, to fly and float and dance in unison with everything and everyone because we are all connected.

Realities become more energetic and again dream like. In our dreams we experience a holographic reality that we may think it isn't real but in fact it is. Everything exists at some level whether we are able to perceive it or not.

We start to utilize our dreams for many different purposes; clearing "past and future" timelines", anchoring more Light are just a few examples. The more we anchor our pure Soul/Light inside the more we are connecting to the 5D/New Earth grids that already exist in our planet and then get ready because realities will never be the same. You will start to have more synchronicities, more miracles, magic and blessings, things will pop out of what seems "nowhere", the possibilities and opportunities are endless and you'll be able to shift in and out of dimensions at will.

As your body becomes Light you let go of the density that kept you bound to a reality with fixed rules, set boundaries, endless limitations and countless boxes, too small for your Soul to fit in. This becomes a whole new way and the freedom we achieve as we continue to anchor more Light and honor our LightBody fully is very different from the experiences we had in the old days. So keep opening up and listening/honoring your LightBody in every way because the more you do the more it will support you in getting out of the 3D prison cells.

APPRECIATE

There is an energy that we begin to hold as we integrate more Light and it is appreciation; a deep sacred appreciation for everything and everyone. The more we see just how everything is linked, intertwined and supportive of our journey in more ways than we thought we start to fully appreciate it, we thank it and become deeply grateful for it. At first it may take awhile as we all have had to endure deep traumatic realities that leave us shaken up but when we open up more and feel every bit of emotion with our whole being, we start to see the purposes that *that* experience served.

Our Soul chose every major experience in our life, it knew that it would serve a purpose; it knew that it would assist in its soul evaluation and growth. Now all of our karmic experiences that we chose do serve a purpose until we start to become more conscious and remember that we no longer need to play in the karmic games anymore. We break free from the karmic loops, patterns and cycles the more we start to regain full consciousness of who we are and what our Soul purposes are. When we expand our consciousness we get to remember why we chose certain people and certain realities in this existence and how they have supported us in waking up. This is when we start to see the bigger picture in all and we start to release and dissolve all of the pain, judgment, suffering and hatred.

Every single experience was meant to trigger all of these deeply suppressed emotions in one way or another so that we can free ourselves from them. When we can appreciate every person, every experience, every reality and every Soul choice we get to have a completely different reality. We are no longer bound by our ego perceptions and victim mentalities, we no longer keep those old memories and realities alive, we innerstand their role, we appreciate every person that honored their agreement to play that specific role and you open yourself up so that you can become fully free from that experience.

The "Past"

The more you allow yourself to feel everything associated with the perceived "past", the more you allow yourself to be fully free from it. Many people believe that you cannot change the "past" but yet you can; you can change the way you perceive it, they way you see it, the way you describe it, the way it affected you, the way in which it supported you in your awakening to remembering more of who you are. It may have not seem like it supported you at the time because of the physical, emotional and mental trauma/separation that it may have caused in that moment but nothing is irreversible. This becomes each and every person's responsibility to break free from the perceptions that we once held towards that heavy experience that at a Soul level we chose. When you are able to change how you see it, how you perceive it, how you describe it, you can change how it affected you. If we keep repeating the same old story, we keep recreating that same scenario never breaking free from the heaviness of it and we only amplify it in ways that it creates more density and emotional attachment towards it.

We must allow ourselves to continuously open up to feel everything associated with this experience in a sacred space where we can feel loved and supported and where our bodies can fully relax throughout the releasing process. The emotional suppression of it keeps one bound to it, reliving it, recreating it, re experiencing it in our reality over and over and over. You have the ability to set yourself free from it by choosing to feel, say, express and connect with every aspect that felt it did not get to feel, say and express everything that it was feeling inside at the moment it occurred. This creates an opportunity for your body/mind to fully release all the discordant frequencies held inside that kept you bound to that reality. It's a process, it is part of this journey and remember that it can take time to fully process and release all the layers and layers of suppressed energy but keep opening up and talking yourself into it because this will allow you to no longer keep it inside.

The full release of these energies and frequencies allows you to see this experience from a completely and totally different angle and perspective. You stop judging it, you stop hating it, you stop pushing it away or disowning it. When you release yourself from it it doesn't mean that you pretend it didn't happen, instead you are able to recognize why it happened and how it was an important part of your journey. If the story and details are appropriate in assisting others in their journey then yes we share what we feel called to and guided but we don't keep sharing and retelling the story over and over because we don't need to and we do get to a point where we don't need to share any of the details because we reach a space inside where we fully clear it all from the body and so at some level it doesn't even exist anymore. A lot of the times when we do feel guided to share our old 3D experiences we utilize different words and we have a completely different energy towards it because we have come to a place inside where we appreciate it.

There is a higher and bigger purpose in everything we choose to experience here. There is no accidents, no mistakes, no misfortunes for everything is connected to the greater picture and everything supports us in one way or another. If you choose to continually open your heart and mind to it all you'll start to feel/sense it all and you'll always come to innerstand and appreciate absolutely everything in your reality.

RESPECT

Respect is a big aspect of this journey as well. Not only do we come to respect ourselves more for who we are and what we came here to do but simultaneously we also come to respect every other being and energy on this planet.

In the old days we didn't fully innerstand this energy and how to apply it because the old 3D world has no respect for our purity, it does not respect our Soul/Light, it doesn't respect nature, Gaia and all the beings living on her. The 3D matrix reality is held on and created by the most deeply unconscious aspects of ourselves and so therefore it functions in pretty much the same way. It emotionally controls and manipulates others, it thrives on competition and creating more separation in every way, it creates rules and law that are all based on protection and survival mechanisms, it creates more fear and separation and propagates war, distortion, suffering across the planet and much more.

When you start to break free from the lower realms you start to reverse everything and you start to respect yourself, by listening, supporting, loving, embracing and accepting every aspect of who you are no matter what. We start to respect ourselves more than the old ways and systems, we start to pave our own way and our own path and create a different reality for ourselves. This is where we start to anchor more into our 5D/New Earth reality. In these higher realms we come to respect everything in a whole new way.

Everything that we do, say, share must be highest align and must respect who we are and where everyone is as well. We don't demand, force or convert, anyone to do anything because we would be disrespecting their Soul choice. Even when we can see how much painful an experience or a thought/belief or choice can bring someone we must be able to fully honor and respect their Soul choice even if their human is still deeply unconscious. As a Soul we innerstand that everyone has already chosen their path, we aren't here to carry, save, sacrifice in any way because we would be going against their Soul chosen path. If the human becomes more conscious of their choices and chooses to break free and receive support, then we tune in and assist as guided in an appropriate way so that we can continue to honor the agreement we have with that Soul.

Honor

Our Soul contracts and agreements are to be honored no matter how difficult it may be for our human to act those out. When we become more conscious of our roles and we start to shift, complete or upgrade our Soul contracts and we start to have a much more evolved and Soul aligned experience with people in our reality that may or may not be conscious or awake yet. That's the beauty of being conscious and aware, that when we recognize our Soul contracts we can choose to end/complete these contracts by honoring our Soul/Light in creating an experience that is much more peaceful and graceful. This may take much, much clearing and dissolving in our part depending on the relationship we have with the person we have the Soul contract with.

When we are able to clear and complete our contracts we can evolve and upgrade them to an agreement; these are much more malleable, bendable and they are not karmic. It becomes a much more enjoyable experience to have and again it allows one to come into a deeper sense of appreciation for that person that honored their Soul contract with you and now that you have learned the lessons and balanced out the energies your experience/interaction with that said person will be a totally different one.

It truly doesn't matter where each person that we come in to contact is in their journey because it is all about the energies/emotions we hold inside that truly matter. When we are able to recognize them, own them, feel them fully and release them, we get to experience a reality where we can fully honor and respect one another as a Soul instead of continuing to feed the ego and creating more karmic/imbalanced realities.

Again it truly boils down to a continual return to full honor and respect towards ourselves, all that we are, and all that we've been so we can have that same level of honor and respect towards others and at the same time receive that from others as well.

LISTEN

Everything is energy and as so it is always vibration, sending off frequency waves of information. Because of how shut off our bodies have been we haven't been able to fully listen to and open up to this frequency. As you continue to open up and reconnect back with your body, Soul, heart you will start to open up and receive more information from all around. This information opens us up to more knowledge, more wisdom, more awareness of everything that affects us, how it affects us and it gives us the keys to be able to make the necessary choices so we can start to shift and realign everything.

For many of us one of the things that also kept us closed and shut off from listening is the fear of knowing too much, becoming aware of truths that we didn't want to hear, and what this new awareness will require us to do. Our egos get stuck in the head conjuring scenarios and circumstances that create more fear and so we end up consciously and unconsciously shutting our ears in many ways so that we don't listen.

Remember that awareness is key, the more we start to open up and see/feel things as they are the more we are able to do something about them. It may seem scary at first but keeping ourselves stuck, stagnant because we are afraid of the perceived "future" or the choices we may have to do in the "future" only holds us back from creating a different reality for ourselves. It is in opening up and truly listening that we start to gain more information and not only would we receive more information that could free us but we would also be opening up so our bodies can guide us in the necessary steps that we would need to take in order to move forward.

Our Bodies

Our bodies are always communicating with us whether we are conscious of it or not, they know the ins and outs of everything that goes on inside and when there is a disturbance or imbalance it tries its best to realign it and bring it back to balance. However the body is not alone, it comes with our conscious mind that at first it blends in with our ego aspects. These aspects are disconnected from the body and so they can't listen to what it is saying. It is only when we start to quiet the mind, dissolve our ego aspects, allow ourselves to open up fully to our body that we start to listen and have a two way communication that will support our journey.

There are parts of our journey where pain and discomfort is the body showing us where we hold a lot of density that needs to be cleared in order for the body to restore back its natural flow. We are so used to resorting to a health professional or someone "outside" of ourselves for answers because we don't trust ourselves or our bodies enough to let us know what is going on. If you open yourself to your body and fully listen and surrender to what it is saying you will start to experience and much "easier" journey. I say "easier" because it will still test your ego and it isn't easy for the ego because it goes against everything it believes in, but in the long run if you listen to your body and follow its guidance you will be supporting it more than you know and eventually you learn to not feed into the egos fears anymore.

You don't need to be a professional or an expert on health or biology or human anatomy, the only thing to remember is to just keep opening up to your body, keep listening and keep doing everything you are guided so that you can return to trusting it. The body knows exactly what you need to do in order to support the massive amount of upgrades, repairs, clearing that it is trying to do and so the less you fear it and the more you embrace and honor it the smoother the process will be.

As you continue to expand and upgrade physically the body will go through normal phases of clearing and expansion where it will be uncomfortable, painful and you will feel discomfort and that is what I call "growing pains." Your whole entire body is stretching, expanding in ways that we never experienced before and so just like you went through the leg pains when growing up the clearing and expansion process feels very much the same.

Again, don't fear the weird, bizarre and painful sensations because it is only the body trying to do an enormous amount of upgrading in order to allow your Soul/Light to come back inside of your body.

Your Environment

The more you connect and listen to your body the more connected you will be to everything around you. Everything is connect to you, everything holds a frequency and so when you are open enough to tune in to your environment you will start to feel how your body reacts or responds to it. Sometimes you will open up and relax and soften and sometimes you may have the opposite reaction and it is important to become aware of each as this will clue you in to whether your surroundings are supporting you or diminishing you.

This is where you start to take responsibility of everything that is around you so that you can bring more of that or remove it completely so that your body no longer is affected by its frequency. This takes constant tuning in, constant listening, constant moving and opening so that you stay continuously connected to all that is around you. Eventually you start to realize that everything around you is meant to support you and so you are no longer attached to anything but deeply and sacredly connected to all where you can recognize its purpose and aren't attached emotionally when that particular object or even person no longer serves a higher purpose in your reality. We honor it and appreciate but we easily remove/shift it out of our reality in the ways that are highest aligned.

Words and Energy

Our whole body becomes a receptor and a transmitter and so when we hear words, energy or any frequency we start to not only listen with our ears but listen with our entire bodies. We no longer listen to just the words that are being said but we feel/sense the energy behind the words. It is quite fascinating because as you open up more and more you will start to feel people more, know where they are coming from, tune in to the level of consciousness in which they are operating and you will come to do the same thing for yourself.

You will start to observe and feel the energy behind what you say, the tone you say it in, your shift in frequency and so much more. You start to recognize that you may use certain words with certain people that are connected to a certain level of consciousness and with others you may feel more comfortable using different words, it is quite fascinating. This becomes a tool you use to gauge where you are not to judge anything or anyone but it is just an opportunity to you to recognize where you are coming from by tuning in to the words and the energy behind the words that you are saying.

So many of us are so unconscious of the words we use and when we start to listen to ourselves more we can start to see why we are experiencing certain things in our realities. This is where words, thoughts and behaviors are very important to become aware of because if you are really in tune inside and "out" you can start to feel how the energy behind these is truly creating a reality that you may or may not want. By feeling all that you still have inside and then by starting to shift your words you will start to have a completely different experience, one that is not feeding the old fear based mentalities, one that is not connected to the old 3D structures and yes you will start to utilize different words that are more in alignment with the reality that you want to experience.

Keep opening up, tuning in inside and listening to everything around you so that you can continue to shift in the ways that are highest align for you so that you can start to experience a New Earth Now in every way.

FOLLOW

There is an important part of the process where we have to follow our inner guidance, our Higher Self guidance instead of letting our ego aspects control our reality. We stop following other people's advice, other people's belief systems and instead we start to listen to our bodies, our LightBodies, our hearts and follow them in every way.

One of the easiest ways to start doing this is to detach from the old world, disconnect from anything and anyone that is still operating from a 3D level of consciousness. We get to a point where being on your own, by yourself, without the influence, approval or distraction from the "exterior" world makes things a lot easier. The "outside" world no longer serves us in the ways it once did and so we come to fully unanchor from it in every way that we are guided. We start to no longer feed it, we no longer engage with it, our relationships start to change and so many other things. This is a normal and important part of the process because we start to remove all "outside" influences and we start to listen to ourselves, we start to tune in deeper to our bodies, our hearts, our Soul and the stronger the connection becomes the more you'll be able to stand in your truth and follow your Higher Self with more and more confidence.

Many people may or may not fully innerstand, agree or believe in our choices but that becomes less and less relevant the more and more we continue to listen, honor and follow our inner guidance. For far too long we believed that our "external" world had the answers and this made us slowly lose trust in ourselves, our bodies, our heart until we stopped listening all together. This is about regaining trust and communication with all that we have inside. As our LightBodies start to come more and more online we start to gain access to our inner knowledge and this opens us many things for us.

LightBody

The LightBody is Divine Intelligence, it has the ability to process information at the speed of light but because our bodies were so dense all this information was dormant and buried under layers and layers of old programs and systems. Our DNA has the capacity to store an enormous about of information, far greater than our linear minds can hold but since our DNA was shut off and disconnected none of us had access to any of it. As our LightBody starts to come online and clears more and more density, our DNA starts to recode itself and our junk/dormant DNA starts to activate so that we can start to gain access to more of our internal sacred knowledge.

It is true that all the answers lie inside and this is mainly because the amount of information that your body is able to hold is far greater than what we thought. Our bodies know exactly what it needs to heal, repair, support, clear, cleanse, unify and even though it's been trying to do this since we incarnated our linear minds and all the programming that gets instilled inter-fears with the process. The old reality has set rules, it has limited perceptions, it labels everything, it puts everything in neat little boxes and if anything falls outside of any of these things it doesn't know what to do, it creates more labels, more boxes, more limits and restrictions creating more fear, lack and judgment.

Our bodies feel the density and heaviness of it all and it tries to communicate with us in more ways than we have been consciously aware of. In the old days, when we had pain or discomfort it was our bodies way of showing us that there was a block or imbalance in that part of the body. This is true still but now all the Light that is entering our bodies is clearing all that stuff out of the body so that it can make space for more Light to come through.

The world is changing fast and we must be open and willing to follow what our bodies already know. Our bodies are aware of all the density and they are assisting us in opening up to allow more Light through. Light is who we are and the more Light we hold inside of our bodies the more we can change our reality, the more our experiences become a reflection of all that we are as Light and pure Love. It will continuously be more and more important for all of us to let go of the old ways and start to really listen and follow our Soul/Light. Yes, it's not an easy thing at first because of all the fears and programming that we have but the more you allow yourself to feel it fully the more you break free from it and the easier it will be to start following your inner guidance more and more until it becomes second nature.

Going Against the Old

Sometimes it will be challenging to follow our Soul because it will make us go against the old but this is what we are all going to have to do at some point. This is part of our purpose and mission coming down here; we see the old, we feel it all and then we shift all that energy within ourselves so that we can then create a new everything. It is important to see the old, all of the old programming that we functioned from because being aware then allows us the opportunity to have a choice, we can then choose to do, be, respond differently and therefore create a whole new reality for ourselves. Yes, it takes guts, boldness, courage and so much more but the more we hold our Light we get to stand up for the new in a whole new way as well. The old ways of yelling, fighting, protesting is something we break away from because our energy speaks louder than anything else. In many cases, we learn to break free from the old in ways that aren't loud or aggressive but rather quiet and soft at times.

We follow our own inner calling no matter what and at the same time respect everyone else's point of view, beliefs or judgments. We are no longer affected by other's thoughts or views; we see them and stand tall in our own inner guidance because we know that at some point when they are ready they will have to do the same thing. Yes, we are the

WayShowers and we chose to come down here to be the first ones to go against the old rules so that others can also start to wake up to their own inner guidance and follow it as well. In many different aspects others have to see other people doing it so they can work up the courage and energy to do it themselves in their own lives; it's almost like we give others permission to follow their heart and inner truth. This is how we all affect and influence one another, by being the example, by walking the walk and showing people that there is a different way, a different reality that already exists, we don't have to sit and wait for the world to change because if we do then we will never see the world change the way we want, we must be the change first and always because then and only then can that change actually be seen and experienced in each person's reality.

More and more of us are starting to feel a deep inner calling to go a different route, live a different way, do different things, be in different places, engage in what they actually love not in what society thinks we should do based on the financial security that its perceived to create. We are waking up to a whole new world and reality that no longer fits and no longer works anymore and we must be willing to open up to changing every aspect of our reality that creates fear and stress. Our bodies are no longer going to be able to maintain and sustain these old realities, they are waking up, they are being activated and they are pushing everything up to the surface so you can feel it, sense it and no longer carry it around with you. Everything that creates heaviness, creates a distraction or a fear that must be removed from your reality so that your LightBody can live surrounded by the things that actually support it. We have lived far too long with things and relationships that created more fear and chaos and that will continue to grow collectively and globally until we take action and remove it ourselves physically while also allowing our Light to clear it at an energetic and cellular/DNA level.

Keep opening up your heart, body, mind so that you can continue to listen and follow the guidance steps so that you can experience a whole new word for yourself. You don't have to follow the old anymore, you don't have to fear it or succumb to it anymore because it is collapsing more and more. The more you take yourself away from experiences that support the old and start to realign your entire reality the more you will no longer have physical experiences that feed into your fear/lack based mentalities.

You are not alone in this journey and you never have, all you have to do is remind yourself in every way that the New is fully supportive of who you are and that the more you follow your inner/Soul guidance the entire Universe will align experiences, people, things, opportunities that will support your journey in every way.

LEAD

    As LightKeepers and WayShowers, we lead in a whole new way, we herald the New Earth realities that we each birth within ourselves. In many cases we get to create, bring, share all new ways of doing that don't conform with the old and yes it may take "time" for others to really get the bigger picture but we don't really care about "time" anymore, we just listen, we follow and that in itself is leading and making way for a whole new world. We no longer wait for other's to show us, show up, lead, direct, we become it all, we become our own leader as a Higher Self by following its voice, guidance and direction. It is a simultaneous process that occurs, the more we follow our own Higher Self aspects we become the NEW leaders in many ways.

    Our old leadership is crumbling and collapsing faster than we can perceive it and so the old people, the old voices, the old rules that we used to follow no longer apply. We used to believe that we needed to follow their lead because we weren't taught how to follow our own, how to trust our own, or even believe that we had the answers ourselves; we are finally breaking free from following the old and fully trusting in our own inner and Higher Self voice. It takes much practice of course because it is scary and a bit frightening at first because it is so much easier to just follow the crowd, follow the old, follow those that we perceive are better or smarter or stronger than us. Our ego aspects live in hiding, they live perceiving themselves to be weak, small and powerless and so they draw their energy from others, they cling and hang on to the old because they are so afraid of actually coming out and becoming the leader they fear.

For most of us the energy behind leadership is that of a distorted sense of power, control and manipulation and so we have to feel it all, confront and own up to everything we still feel and believe about becoming a leader. Everything will come up to the surface for you to feel and it's suppose to, allow it, don't fear it anymore, it is time for you to feel and release everything that is still holding you back from becoming the pure version of yourself that you really are so that you can save yourself from the old. Yes, no one is going to save you, carry you, or spoon feed you anymore because this isn't our role, this isn't how we all claim our true sovereignty and power, we all have to let our old ego aspects die and dissolve so that we can rise up as pure Light.

This is where we get to "prove" and create a whole new version of leadership, one that is nothing like the old, one that honors and respects, values and embraces, cares and uplifts every single human being and energy in this planet for who it actually is not from what the old world perceived it to be based on the old constructs. We become the Light leaders by leading and creating our own reality. This is about fully owning up to everything we have ever created in every single one of our existences and no longer hiding, blaming, shaming or judging it; we see it all for what it is, take responsibility and shift the energy ourselves. This is how we rebirth ourselves and become Masters of our energy, our reality and our world and in that role we get to lead others in doing the exact same thing. We are not here to create a dependency anymore, that was the old ways, we came here to show and support each and every person on this planet so that they can become their own leader, their support system, their best supporter and their own creator of their reality.

Empowering each and every person is part of what we are all here to be and do in many different ways and so open up to that. The more Light you hold, the more you'll start to remember this and the more you'll start to take full responsibility for all that you came here to be and do and show and share. This is how we activate and remind more and more people of who they are, by being it ourselves and just sharing it, not forcing it down people's throat, not diminishing people, not forcing or converting like in the old ways, we aren't here to bring people down but uplift people in all that they are and all that they can be. Be the follower of your Light and the leader of Light so that we can create a world full of Light, peace, hope and pure Love in every way.

ENCOURAGE

Many of us were brought up in an environment that did not uplift, encourage or provided the energy that we needed, in fact it is like that for every single one of us no matter how you or others perceived your upbringing to be, that really doesn't matter because we all signed up to carry an enormous amount of fear, distortions and heaviness so we can learn/remember how to shift it all back into Light. This is where each and every single person must be that which we needed growing up. We need to become the person that encourages, uplifts, supports and cheers us on in every step of the way so that we can have the energy and strength to continue.

I say this sometimes in my own videos as I am guided, this journey is not always rainbows and unicorns, I mean it is but it isn't, we all have to feel an enormous amount of emotions that are beyond what we have experienced in the past and that is all a huge part of this process so that we can release and dissolve it all and no longer carry it. And so yes there will be times that you will want to throw the towel, give up, quit, forget about it all and it is in those moments that you have to open your heart even more and allow your Higher Self aspects to come through and bring you the encouragement you need. In a way it is you encouraging yourself, you loving on yourself, and reminding yourself that you're loved and supported above all things; things will get better, you will get through this because you have the energy and strength already inside, you just have to keep activating it and keep holding it so you can become it.

Every kind of encouragement we didn't receive growing up we now have to give that to ourselves. It isn't going to be anyone else's job to do this because no one can replace the Light that you are, it is your Light/Soul that can fulfill that role in ways that no one else will ever be able to. This is where we start to remember that everything we ever wanted and needed is already inside and now as we become more and more conscious we start to become those roles that will support us in this journey.

As you navigate this journey, many inner/wounded aspects of yourself will come up to the surface for you to see and hold space for. These aspects are still living and holding on to the memories, emotions, experiences where they felt like they weren't loved, accepted, supported, wanted and cared for. Every aspect of ourselves that still lives in separation, in the pain and the hurt will come up to the surface so that you can allow this aspect to feel everything that it is still holding on. This aspect just needs the space, freedom and love in which to let it all out and it needs you to be there with it, nobody else but you. As you continue to open up your heart you will start to realize that the love you can provide and hold for each of these aspects is enough, your Light is enough, your pure love is enough all you have to do is give yourself permission to be with these aspects and no longer hide from them, run away from them or fear all that is still yet to be felt. Let go of fearing the fear or the emotional experience because there is nothing to be afraid anymore, you don't have to fear anything anymore because it is only an aspect of yourself that wants to be seen, it wants your attention, it needs you to let go of the judgment, resentment and just be with it, just connect with it and you'll start to see/feel/remember how powerful that actually is.

Divine Mom and Dad

No one on this planet has experienced the frequencies of the Divine Mother and Father in its entirety growing up. Not to say that we didn't get glimpses or the opportunity here and there because I know we did if we open our hearts and remember. Our human parents played an important role in our reality that we pre-chose before coming here and now as we start to become more conscious we realize that the frequencies of the Divine Mother/Feminine and Divine Father/Masculine are right inside each and every single one of us. We must become this energy, hold it and share it so we can also align with experiences and people that will reflect that back to us.

As we become this pure frequency inside and start to encourage ourselves through these Divine Aspects we start to dissolve a lot of the emotional heaviness, cords and attachments that we had toward our human parents and family too. We start to see things differently, we start to remember their roles and purposes and even why we chose them, why we chose the experiences we had and how they all were triggers and activators of our Soul in many ways but we just didn't know it at the time. We let go of the self blame, shame, guilt and judgment and no longer hold on to the blocks and cords that we believed we needed to hang on to. We give ourselves permission to be free, to live without remorse or judgment of what we perceived happened in those old times and moments; we innerstand that the only person that we were harming or hurting by holding on is ourselves no one else and so the more we start to see ourselves for all that we are, see those aspects of ourselves that only wanted and needed love we come to have a deep sense of honor and love so we can return all of our inner/wounded child aspects back into our heart.

As we continue to ascend our Divine Mother and Father frequencies become more and more activated in every way. We then bring these aspects forward in any and every situation as needed so that we can receive the purity of their love, support, encouragement in every way. The more we receive that from ourselves as these Higher Self aspects we have the beautiful opportunity to then share it and become that for others so that they can also feel/sense these frequencies. The way that we used to share, love and support was all coming from our own sense of lack and so it didn't come from a pure place inside and it just kept creating more lack because the people whom we shared it with did not and could not reciprocate it and so this created a loop cycle in which we felt we weren't good enough, we felt we weren't supported by others and it created more emptiness and lack inside.

When we become the ones that start supporting, loving and encouraging ourselves first in every way and in every aspect it is then and only then that we can share this energy with others without ever expecting anything in return. What we do and share comes from a wholeness and purity inside, unlike the old days where what we did and shared came from a place of neediness, where we wanted or expected something back and we never got it. The more we fill ourselves up with who we already are as Light, the more we start to feel, receive and experience a whole new way of loving. We become this pure Love and we gift ourselves this love in every way, every day in every moment of our existence; this is how we become more and more whole, pure and complete. It is much simpler than we thought, and it doesn't cost anything all we have to do is decide and start to choose it more and more and more.

SIMPLE

There is such a profound and magical simplicity in the purity that we hold. In the old days everything was complicated, intricate, twisted and backwards, it kept us busy, occupied, distracted, unfocused, separated, stressed and closed off to ourselves. The "outside" world become our life, what we did, what we wore, what we ate, who we engaged with, what we achieved, who we became all was part of the distraction game that kept us from fully remembering what really mattered in our lives. We become so preoccupied with financial security, material gains, physical achievements, personal accomplishments, always reaching for the next goal, promotion, title, degree and so much more that only holds importance in the old world. All of these things created looping cycles, cords of attachments and separated us from going deeper inside. We thought that in order to be successful, acclaimed, valuable we needed to prove it, we needed to become who we thought the world wanted us to be in order to live and survive and yet all with a cause. Whether we know it, belief it or not, we sold ourselves, we sold our Soul to the ways and rules of the old world, creating a reality that only benefitted the old systems and beliefs instead of ourselves and our LightBodies.

As you start to feel more, you start to become aware of how things in your reality bring more stress and chaos in your world and this is important. We must become conscious and start to feel how everything affects our reality in every way and own up to it. If we keep suppressing or denying it nothing will every change and the more stuck and stagnant things will become that will be detrimental in every aspect of our being, emotionally, mentally, physically and energetically. The wonderful thing is that everything is becoming very loud right now, things are becoming bold and blatant; all that isn't working anymore and isn't bringing us peace of mind is becoming more and more noticeable and this is an amazing opportunity for change. Change starts with each person, it starts within, inner change is the only thing that can create lasting change in our reality because it is inside that everything is created from; it isn't from some "outside" force, in fact it is coming from that force but from within because you are that perceived "outside" force, you are everything, there is no separation at all.

We you start to remember this and connect with all aspects of yourself you start to feel the beauty, the peace and the love from just BEing. You recognize that everything that kept you busy and distracted only created more separation from that which you hold inside that is simple and pure. This is where magic starts to occur because the more you can feel the deep sacred love that you are and the more you remember that you don't need a lot of the stuff you thought you needed you become aware of how stressful your life really is. The things you thought you needed to achieve, have, be, accomplish, attain all just created more stress, it didn't bring lasting peace like maybe you thought they would. It is in that moment of pure remembrance that you start to let those things go, they just don't matter anymore, they don't hold the same value as they once did and you start to focus more on what actually does, you, your Light, your body, your mental/emotional/physical/energetic health. Nothing becomes more important than all that you are and so you consciously start to bring everything back into a space of peace and simplicity.

Things don't have to be complicated in fact if they are complicated then we are resisting, fighting and trying to make a square peg fit into a round hole, it's just not possible, and all we are really doing is exerting an enormous amount of energy that sucks our Light and is exhausting. When we realize that everything is energy, everything is always moving and shifting and that we are this energy then in order to create things we must become this energy first and then the steps we need to take become a synchronistic dance and flow that brings no resistance at all. The old world complicated things because this is how it took energy out of us. The systems, program, foundations with lots of rules, regulations, laws, mandates were only meant to create more fear, lack, resistance, push, control inside of us and this energy is the exact energy that kept those systems a live through, quite fascinating in a way but so twisted and backwards. The more we are involved in the systems the more of this energy we output that sustains and feeds them.

As we start to fully go all in on this journey, releasing, feeling, clearing, anchoring more of our Light we start to not give into these systems anymore. We start to create a beautiful, simple flow in our realities which allows us to no longer be affected by those "outside" systems. In many ways we do have to detach and unanchor any emotional attachment we have with them so that when we do have to come into contact or engage with them our experience is actually one that is simple, open and expansive. It is truly the Light that we hold that makes the difference. I had an experience last year where I had to get my license and even though at one point I was resistant about going back and engaging with these systems I was able to release so much of the heaviness inside that when it got time to go to the establishment and go through the process, I was able to observe everything from a much expanded stance, I held my Light, I went with the flow, I created that peace inside and held on to the frequencies of simple, ease and grace and the experience was exactly that. Everything flowed and even when I got a bit triggered, I went back to my center and continue to hold my Light and after that it was easy breezy. These kinds of experiences allow you to see so much and gift you the opportunity to really feel how powerful we truly are and even while these systems are still operating and we might have to engage with them we don't have to succumb or feed into them the way that they expect us too, the way that it feeds them but quite the opposite and it is truly profound.

The more you allow yourself to realign, reorganize, reevaluate everything in your life so that you can have more peace and clarity the more simple life becomes. Life isn't supposed to be complicated at all, yes it will bring its challenges but that is because our ego is so stubborn and strong that it challenges us, it challenges our belief systems, our programming, our fears so that we no longer have to be controlled by them. And after we open up and expand and go with the flow things become simple, magical and pure. We no longer have to engage in things that are complicated because we thought that doing those things would bring us appraisal or recognition, instead we give ourselves our own appraisal and recognition and then we only choose to engage in those things that are simple yet bring so much fulfillment, love, peace and joy.

Our entire reality is shifting and we must be open to it because it is allowing us to create more simplicity and peace in our lives. We no longer need to live in the stress, the havoc, the chaos, the uncertainty, the fear, the lack, the rat race that we thought we needed to; we don't belong to that world and never have because that is not who we are at our core. The more we feel all that we truly are then we will start to experience a whole new world where peace and magic abound in the most simple and profound ways.

Nature

Our reconnection with nature brings us back to this pure place, it is where we are able to find so much joy and peace in the simple things. We actually don't need much, one because we already hold everything we need inside and all the things that we choose to surround ourselves us that reflect who we are only amplify our Light even more. The beauty and magic of nature, of the elements, of animals activate so much sacred remembrance inside that is beyond what we can find in the old busy world. This is why it is so important and imperative that we continue to spend time, reconnect, support and merge with nature in every way.

Nature already holds the frequency of simplicity, it already exists in this Divine flow and unison with everything around, it holds the keys and codes that assist us in activating that within ourselves so we can return to living in unity, peace and simplicity that brings so much joy and love. If you would gift yourself the opportunity to let go, remove, release yourself from all the noise, distractions, old world expectations, obligations, tasks, responsibilities that only fed our ego/lack mentalities and instead replaced it with more nature time, more nature sounds, more of these pure frequencies in every way possible you will feel, integrate and anchor even more of this into your reality. This is when we become minimalists, we start to purge and remove so many of our physical belongings because we realize that the reason we are keeping them isn't brining more peace but instead taking up much space. As we open up and create more space for ourselves we only allow ourselves to bring in that which supports our Light, opens our hearts, creates more simplicity and peace in every way.

Our merging with nature becomes a necessity and no longer a commodity; it is who we are and so the more space we create for it the more we access our own Divine essence in ways that we never had or never thought we could do. Keep opening yourself up, keep reconnecting with these beautiful frequencies and you'll start to regain trust, unity and respect for all that they hold and bring.

RETREAT

There is a huge part of this phase where we must allow ourselves to retreat, recharge, and replenish ourselves with all that we truly are. There is still much noise, distraction, fear and lack in the old world and in order to create the opposite we have to retreat, detach, unanchor by engaging less and less with it. When you realize that the old world only creates more fear, lack, separation and stress then you will consciously make the necessary choices so that you can create a reality that doesn't feed it, support it or create more of it. This isn't to say that you won't need to continue to engage with it because at some level we do, but that is how we get to hold our Light in a way that nothing "out there" can truly bring us down. The "outer" world may still activate emotions and belief systems held inside and so it still serves a purpose for many including myself but we are no longer bound to it and we no longer live or experience it in the ways that we used to when we were unconscious.

The alone and sacred space that we must continuously create for ourselves is one that is highly important. This is a space where we get to be with all that we are, gift ourselves the love that we need, reconnect with all aspects that we need to reconnect with and bring more of the

Light that we are so we can continuously remind and remember our purposes and roles. It becomes a sacred space that we actually hold and keep inside that we can always return to and feel no matter where we may be physically located. We no longer are bound by a certain location because we become this sacred space always but at the beginning it is a physical location that we go to and as we engage and connect and spend more time in this space the more we activate those frequencies within ourselves where we then become it all.

When we first awaken we must create this physical space for ourselves in whatever way we are guided. At first my bedroom become this space and my backyard, I would spend tons of time here, alone, meditating, connecting, feeling and just being. I now realize the importance that this is in every single one of us especially at the beginning when you start to learn and remember and realize that your entire reality isn't what you thought it was. For many this is quite devastating and hard to grasp and swallow and for me it was in these moments of solitude of being in this space that I started to reconnect more and more with the frequencies and aspects that I needed that supported me throughout this journey.

Lower and Higher Aspects

One of the hugely impactful practices that I created for myself recently is connecting with aspects that were polar opposites. In anything that I was experiencing or feeling I would allow both aspects of myself to come through and release/share/express anything and everything that they needed to. Sometimes my lower selves would come through, yelling, crying, cursing, and I needed to allow them to do this so that they can finally let this energy go. The sacred space that we create greatly assists because when you allow yourself to retreat from the entire world, create a space where you feel safe and supported the easier it will be to let these aspects out and to relax your entire body as this is also a huge part of the process.

Your physical environment plays a huge role and so the more you create an environment where you feel safe and loved and fully supported the more these aspects are going to feel that and the more they are going to openly release everything that they have been holding on to. This is also why not being around anyone is really important many times. Not to say that others can't hold this space for you because they can but one, we can't always depend on someone to be there for us when we are going through these emotional releases and two it is part of bringing ourselves back into our full Mastery where we are able to provide for ourselves everything we need so we can dissolve and resolve all that we may still need to. You want to learn to be by yourself in these moments of deep emotional purge so that you can also gift yourself all the love and support that every aspect needs. It is through loving and honoring yourself and every aspect that you start to have a much deeper, sacred and profound respect and love for yourself and this is what we are all returning to.

When you create this space for yourself physically, "externally" and internally you will be opening up yourself for your Higher Self aspects to also come through in any way that they need to provide the loving support and care that every part of your being needs. When you allow yourself to be by yourself, completely away from anyone else, you are able to hold your Light in a much more powerful way that you previously thought possible. There is so much pure power and strength within and a lot of the times the way we start to activate this deep inside is in those alone and sacred spaces in which it is just us. Many of us still hold a lot of resistance and fear of being by ourselves and this also stems from not actually wanting to be with parts of ourselves that we don't want to look at. We have an unconscious and subconscious fear, disgust and hatred towards many aspects of ourselves that we may not realize and being by ourselves gives us the opportunity to reconnect at a deeper level that we may still fear. This is where creating a space or being in a space where you can fully open up, relax, release and feel more is so crucial, because no matter what aspect of ourselves comes up to the surface we still have the sacred love that surrounds us that will make us feel safe in reconnecting with these aspects.

The more you open yourself up to being in solitude, in a sacred space the more you'll start to feel, sense and remember who you are and the more you'll feel safe enough to let go of everything that you aren't. The more you keep holding on to these frequencies the more you'll be able to share and transmit this for others to feel too in ways that it activates them more and more.

PATIENCE

The energy of patience is one that becomes activated the more we hold our Light. Our Light fills us up to where we no longer experience lack like the way we used. In the old ways when we were controlled by fear and lack, we were impatient, we wanted things instant, quick, fast because somewhere deep inside we held on to the belief that we weren't enough, we weren't perfect and so we needed instant approval, appraisal or gratification. Our bodies held on to so much lack and separation that time and space was seen differently, they were a testament of that which we didn't hold inside. The more lack we held inside the more we believed in the concept of time and separation of space and therefore we pushed and pulled things in order to fill our own void.

Patience takes a whole new meaning the more we start to release and resolve all the separation, the judgment, the fear and lack that we hold at a deep cellular level. Most of these energies we actually don't even know we have because they've been so deeply suppressed that we become numb and immune to them in every level. It isn't until you decide to go all in into your journey that you start to have access and feel so much of the heaviness that still exists inside. The level of awareness and connection that we must all return to is so deep and so sacred and so profound that anything that we have yet to feel becomes very well worthy. There is nothing remotely able to compare to the freedom and expansion that you achieve when you allow yourself to go deeper and deeper and deeeeeeeeeper into the depths of all that you are.

When you open yourself so much you gain access to sacred wisdom and knowledge that supports you in every way. The old constructs and systems seize to exist and you are no longer bound to them or abide by any of them because your Light takes over. The New Earth systems start to build and get anchored into your physical body to where you are able to create a completely polar opposite reality to that which you had created before. The way that it all occurs sometimes may seem "slow" and other times it may seem lighting fast and this is where holding on to your Light in every way allows you to be more patience, appreciative and grateful for all that you are now allowing.

The way that things materialize in your reality all have to do with the gridding systems already in place inside of your body, this has nothing to do with what you think you belief or what your ego wants because the Soul now fully takes over. Sometimes the gridding systems in place don't fully support the materialization of that which you desire and so one must fully allow for them to be built while following and honoring the steps shown by our Higher Self. A lot of the things that we used to want or desire fed our old ego based mentalities and so these no longer play a role in our reality. This is where becoming so very conscious and aware of the intention behind each and every thing that we ask for is crucial because if there is any ounce of ego involved then it will very likely not get it or not receive it in the ways and forms that the ego might expect. When you choose to see, own and dissolve your ego back inside your Light is able to come through and call forth the things that it needs that will support the Lightbody, our journey and Gaia/the planet as a whole. The times are long gone where we can just ask for anything, create anything that was at some level detrimental to others or the planet itself. We are reverting everything we've ever done and created that was impure and that held an imbalance in the energetic field force in any level, some of us call it karma but it is just an imbalance of energy that must be fully restored and rebalanced and this is what we are all doing at some level.

Open yourself up more and more to listening to your Soul and allowing all to come forth without attaching to it, fully letting go of how or when or what it should look like. This is about fully trusting and continuously holding the field for it to all come through in the way that you most need.

SUPPORT

This is such a huge code for each and every single one of us in every way and in every level. None of us received a hundred percent of the support we needed when we most needed it and this is just part of the human experience that we all chose to have. We came here to see everything from all different levels and dimensions so we can all bring it back to Oneness, Unify with all and return to full Source Consciousness.

This journey is all about coming back to full awareness, seeing where we are still holding on to the perceptions of the "past", where we are still hanging on to the emotional pain that was activated in different moments of our experience, where we are living in separation inside and much more. Coming to a space where we can recognize these energies within will allow us to fill those holes, fill the gap, gift ourselves with the love and support that we didn't receive in those moments. When we allow ourselves to keep living from judgment, from our traumas, from our emotional aspects, from our hurt and pain we keep ourselves living in the never-ending loop cycles that keep recreating more and more experiences that match that exact frequency. It isn't until we decide and choose to feel everything that we realize that the heaviness isn't worth carrying anymore, you start to remember that peace and love is truly what you desire at a deep core level. The beauty is that more and more people are waking up to this remembrance, they are choosing differently, they are choosing to open up more, they are choosing things in their lives that support their Light instead of continuing to live the same old ways.

The support that we all need, desire and deserve as Light Beings is inside, it is within each and every single one of us, it doesn't come from "outside" because that is only a reflection of what we hold inside. So if we get stuck in waiting for others to provide the support we want and we don't give that to ourselves first then nothing will every change. The love and support that will start to change things in your reality is the one that you give to yourself. In the old days, we thought that others came first, we believed that giving to others was more important than giving to ourselves, we carried this savior, martyrdom distortion that kept us separated and miserable because as much as we would give to others we just didn't receive the same support we needed. It is only when you stop carrying more about others and instead start focusing on yourself, your Soul, your LightBody, your mental/emotional/physical health that you start to see all the heaviness you held inside. This is truly the time to let go of the old perceptions and beliefs and start to focus on you, start to support you in every level because only when this occurs will you have the space, energy and purity of intent that will allow you to support and uplift others in a much greater and much more profound way than ever before.

Emotional Support

The emotional support that everyone needed growing up was virtually not present in the way that we needed it. Even when we had the most loving and caring parents there was still a gap on how to honor each and every single emotion because up until this point of our modern history no one was truly taught how to deal, resolve and express every single one of the emotions that exist. For this reason everyone learned to suppress, hide, disown, detach from their emotions, this was easier than to feel or deal with them in many occasions and so we all become masters at suppressing. This suppression creates much stress and imbalance in our bodies, it blocks the organic flow, it creates walls that disconnect every cell in our body and it creates a heaviness that starts to become more and more apparent and felt the more we keep stuffing it inside.

Much of this journey if not all of it deals with learning to open up, feel and dissolve all of our internal emotional baggage. Our emotions are the glue that sustains the systems and structures in the body in which create a physical reality that matches those same emotions. The more we open up to feel more and more of our deep heavy emotions the more we allow the muscles in our body to relax and open up so that we can allow the Light of our Soul to come in and rebuild all of these systems at a cellular/DNA level.

The less you suppress, judge or hide behind your emotions the more you literally release yourself from having to carry the weight of them all. Our bodies are Light, they are meant to only carry Light and so the less room we have for our Light, the heavier, denser, traumatic our experiences will be. The more you feel and release yourself from the heaviness the more space you have for the Light to come through. It is all about continuing to be fully open in every way so that everything that is still stuck inside gets activated so that you can honor it, feel it and allow the Light to clear it fully.

The emotional passageway that one must go through as we navigate the 4th dimensional realm of consciousness is a deep heavy one because all of our emotions come to the surface, they have to, we can't carry those over into the heavenly realms because it isn't who we are; the only thing we get to take with us is our bodies and everything that is fully in alignment with our Soul. As you continue to fully feel, release and dissolve your emotions at a deep core level, your Light comes through and expands your body and your consciousness more and more until you reach a point where your body can house more of your Soul. It isn't until you clear and purify every cell in your body that your physical body ascends with you as well and then it's a whole different ball game from there but don't worry you will be fully ready when this occurs.

Providing yourself with the emotional support that you need is going to be a huge part of this process. Create a sacred space for yourself that fully supports you in this process. This is about reconnecting with every wounded, unresolved, separated aspect of yourself in every way and providing them with the emotional support that they need them. Allow them to feel and physically and verbally release their emotions in the way they need to, in the way that they did not get to when they were young. Remember that these aspects of yourself that may seem stuck in another time are actively playing a role in your reality, so even if they may seem aspects of our past if we haven't fully resolved and dissolved them inside then they are still very much present and in many cases we act, behave, respond from this inner wounded aspect; so even if we may be wxz linear years of age, if we have an inner child/aspect that is still feeling any unresolved pain and anger then when these emotions get triggered and activated we revert back to that moment in the perceived past and we act from that same age.

Many of us are starting to see this play out in many ways, more and more people's emotional traumas are being triggered and activated and it is so that they finally deal and resolve it within themselves. Each and every person must be willing to face their fears, face these wounded aspects and feel everything that they still need to fear. Don't fear the fear for it is just trying to show you where you are still holding an old belief system and when you open up to it, reconnect with the aspect that is holding the fear, you allow more of your Soul/Light to come through and restore the peace and clarity that is already within but couldn't be accessed because of the resistance that was covering it up. There isn't anything wrong in feeling a certain way, we aren't bad people if we allow ourselves to feel or admit that we are feeling a certain way, it's just an energy, a frequency that is heavy and discordant and the more you honor it the less it controls you. Just keep allowing yourself, reminding yourself that it is safe to feel fully and continue to let go of anything that says otherwise.

Mental Support

Mental support and awareness has increased in the recent linear years and it is something that more and more people are dealing with more than ever before. The voices in our head are getting louder and louder and part of the reason is because they've been suppressed for far too long. These voices are coming from our wounded/separated aspects of ourselves that are trapped inside. These are the versions of ourselves that for whatever reason did not get the opportunity to express themselves, speak up, feel what they need to feel. In many cases they may sound like something other than ourselves and that is because they are able to morph into other energies that we may think aren't us; we may perceive them as other entities, dark spirits/forces, but yet they are only aspects of ourselves.

If you have seen the movie Moana, it is very much like what happened to Te Fiti, the mother Island. In the movie it shows how she got her heart taken away by Maui and so she turned into Te Ka, referred to as a demon of earth and fire. When we go through much pain and devastation in our reality and we aren't fully able to process, release, feel, resolve all the emotions attached to the experience we shut off/close off our heart and that same aspect of ourselves turns into another version of ourselves that may seem or feel like a completely different aspect of ourselves. Essentially this unloved, unwanted, abandoned aspect is carrying so much hurt, anger and pain that it morphs into something we may perceive as very dark, it's like it gets so consumed by its own pain that it turns "evil". This is what we may refer to as a very dark side of ourselves, that for many we haven't fully owned or connected with.

This aspect of ourselves just needs the love and support that it never received and it is up to each and every one of us to start giving it the support it needs. When I was going through my continual Dark Night of the Ego, so much mental stuff was coming up to the surface that I had no idea I had; I had suppressed my thoughts so much that when I finally gave all my aspects to speak out they would come out with a vengeance. This was so very important for me to allow and honor because I knew that it was just energy that was deeply held and trapped inside and as I connected with each aspect I gave them the sacred space for them to express in whatever way that they needed.

Writing was a huge support as well, I would get my drawing pad and would write and write and write anything and everything that I had to so that I could move the energy out of my system. It didn't matter what the words were, what the emotion or feeling was, nothing mattered but the sacred and loving space that I was providing for each wounded aspect of myself.

This takes full conscious commitment for every single one of us; we aren't here to judge any of our aspects or call them evil or wrong, they just want a space where they can be heard and loved no matter what they say or feel. For most of us we were deeply embedded with the belief that there are things, words, phrases that we shouldn't say, we shouldn't express anger or sadness, we shouldn't cry or wine, we shouldn't think this way or that way.... All of these old rules and belief systems have created such a contradicting energy and resistance force inside in which we grew up very conflicted.

As kids we are very open and honest and real and this is so very normal but yet when we expressed ourselves in any way that was seen as unacceptable we were punished, denied of loved or threatened in some way; we learned that it wasn't safe to express ourselves in the way that we needed to and that we couldn't be ourselves because we might get punished for it. These and many more similar programs get deeply embedded and carried over throughout many existences and it is in this one that we choose to finally clear and resolved them all.

The mental support that we didn't receive in any of our existences is coming to the surface for every single one of us at an increasing and sometimes overwhelming rate. It is finally time for everyone to start honoring all the voices and aspects that are still trapped inside and are yearning to come out. Be with them, connect with them and let all the energy come out in whatever way it is highest and appropriate in that moment. Yes, it is a process that takes "time", but the more you allow yourself to do this the more you will come to a place inside when pure peace can reign. All your Higher Self aspects will start to come through and remind you how loved, supported and beautiful you really are, allow it. Everything that we did not hear when we were growing up will be coming through your Higher Self as you continue to dissolve all of the wounded aspects. You see the suppressed energy held in place by these aspects kept us from truly listening and hearing the pure aspect of ourselves that is so loving, so caring, the one that encourages us, uplifts us and supports us in every way. Again we have to uncover and free ourselves from all the layers and layers of heaviness in order to have more access and a stronger connection with these pure aspects.

As you continue to allow this process to unfold for you, you will start to come to a pure and expansive place inside where you start to see the roles that other people played in your life; you start to remember why you chose the experiences you lived, you start to completely resolve the anger and hurt you had towards your human parents or family, you start to forgive and become whole all on your own and in many cases without having to have a physical exchange with anyone else, it's beyond magical.

This is the power that we hold inside and the magic that comes from going deeper and deeper, opening more and more, reconnecting with everything that is still inside; we get to that point where we no longer have remorse or anger towards anyone because at the end of the day it was just an experience that we all chose to play in….it doesn't define us, it doesn't make us good or bad, it doesn't make us unworthy, it just becomes an expression that our Soul chose prior to incarnating and now we get to balance it all out.

Physical Support

The physical support can come through in many different ways for many. Again no one truly received the kind of support that they needed when growing up and so this whole journey is about reconnecting with every aspect of ourselves that still is yearning for that love and support that they never received. It is up to each and every single one of us to become that support, to be that Divine Mom and Dad figure that is already inside so that we can return to wholeness.

There is a pure and beautiful alchemical reaction that occurs through physical touch. When we are babies we were held, carried, hugged and touched all the time and it supported us so much. The physical confirmation and feeling of being loved, cared for, wanted, honored and accepted is so very much needed no matter what age you are. In fact, there was something I heard a long time ago that when babies aren't touched or held for very long periods of times they can actually transition out of their bodies. That shocked me a bit but yet it felt so true, the physical touch is so super important when we are babies. This of course starts to dissipate more and more as we get older, we may not get that much physical attention or support in ways that we may need. Many times the physical touch and attention gets replaced by an over abundance of material stuff, toys, stuffed animals, and other tangible things. This may be great for awhile but it will never replace the physical support that we need. Sometimes it can be as simple as just spending time with our human family, being there when they need to express an emotion, hugging them and caressing when they may need some extra love and encouragement. All in all there is no physical object that can ever replace the physical/energetic support that one can bring to another.

As we dive deeper into this journey and start to reconnect with our wounded aspects that didn't receive the physical support, it becomes our responsibility and duty to start giving this to ourselves. No one else is going to drop from the sky and do it, I mean energetically it can and in fact, I take that back you are welcome to call on your angels, guides, Higher Self aspects that you need in any moment so that you can feel the love and support that you need. What I meant to say is that we can't sit and wait until our human parents or family "change" and start giving us the love we needed when we were growing up because now as adults we take charge, we start giving that to ourselves. The beauty and magic in that is that when we start to love and support ourselves more we actually start to receive more of that same love and support from our human family in the ways that we actually need it. It's like when we give ourselves permission to support ourselves in every way our human family and friends become a mere reflection of that and they actually start to change in the most miraculous ways.

Open up to this physical support. For me it has come through being more present with my body, loving it, caring for it, massaging it and caressing it, speaking to it in a pure way and even bringing physical things or even toys that would physically support it. When we talk to our bodies we are actually talking to our inner child, open up to this: how would you talk to a scared, wounded, abandoned child? Remember this when you talk to your body.

The more you connect with your body as these aspects the more you'll start to feel the pain and hurt and if you just sit with it, honor it and feel it in any way that you are guided your body will start to release it. When you open up to your body and open up your heart your Higher Self aspects are going to come through more easily and they will start to bring messages of love, support, encouragement and anything else that your lower self aspects still needs to hear.

This becomes this beautiful whole-ing (becoming whole and complete) experience when we fully allow it.

MELT

There is a profound sensation of melting that occurs when you allow yourself to fully and totally relax. I've mentioned how relaxing is a huge deal in this entire process, not only do your muscles need to relax but your entire mind and body. Your entire body, primarily the muscles hold the grids of everything that makes up your physical reality. Everything from thoughts, thought forms, emotions, programs, memories and belief systems are physically and energetically held inside of your physical body. Are you starting to you see the connection between your body and your reality a little bit more? The old 3D systems were constructed under much fear, lack, judgment, separation that kept our hearts closed, our muscles tight, our body contracted, our fields small and our minds under deep stress. The more we start to open up and fully relax our bodies and fields the more we start to open and release everything.

The physical processes that occur for a full body and cellular release are vast and complex and you will start to feel it. Your body will start to become more relaxed, your mind will become less stressed, your muscles less tight and you'll be able to notice more when you do go back to a contracted space. A lot of people start to become more sensitive and it is important to remember that sensitive is part of who we are. In the old days we used to believe that being sensitive was being too emotional or too easily triggered emotionally. This evolves as you continue to dissolve more and more emotions; when your body is no longer physically carrying an enormous amount of emotional suppression you no longer get emotionally triggered like before. Not to say that you will never be emotionally triggered because that's not the case but when we do become activated in this way we will be able to not let our emotions control our actions like in the old days.

Physical Melt

The first time I started to physically experience what I like to call the melting phase was with my neck. Throughout my entire existence here I have had many times in which my neck would become so incredibly tight that I wasn't able to turn my head for days. Many years later I learned just how much programming is held on our neck and shoulders that explained just how much we have to clear around this area.

As I continued to clear more of my deep suppressed emotions my entire physical structures began to relax more and more to the degree that at one point my neck had no strength at all. My teacher Lisa talks about this and she's shared how she had to wear a neck brace during that phase. I had to buy a neck support pillow myself because when those deep melting experiences happened I had to have something around my neck so that I can just let it melt and have no need to hold it up when I didn't need to.

The muscular strength that was valued in the old days becomes less and less of a goal. We no longer have the desire, energy or need to engage in the old muscular exercises because we start to realize that all the tight muscles in our body led to our tight, fixated and distorted realities of the old 3D world. All of the heaviness inside becomes more anchored the more our muscles are tight and rigid when we function from an unconscious state. I know in the old world our values our different, we believed that our bodies needed to look a certain way, be a certain size, eat certain foods and yet all of this was based on the old belief systems.

There is a phase of the journey where you start to care more about your body, you have the desire to work out more, eat healthier, move more and that is an important place to be. When you go all in on your ascension journey your LightBody starts to come online and its needs become opposite of what our human body needed. When you start to open up to your Light, your muscular strength starts to diminish and we are ok with this. We start to realize that our pure power doesn't come from our muscular strength but rather our Light. The more Light we hold the more we are able to change our reality in the most powerful ways without needing to have the physical muscular strength anymore.

Our bodies begin to dissolve the muscle tightness and this is where the melting experiences start to come online. When our muscles start to feel sore and achy we aren't able to function like we used to function in the old days and this is important. Our bodies start to seem like they are weakening and in a way it may be perceived that way because we start to not have as much energy or we aren't able to do the same things we used to do before. This isn't to say that we won't have any physical strength anymore because we actually do get to and sometimes even more than before. When our muscles are filled with pure Light they are able to breathe, bend and move easier and in a much easier flow.

The lack of energy that we experience happens for many reasons but a lot of the times our bodies and muscles knock us down so we no longer engage in things that no longer serve our Light/LightBody. The more our Light activates inside the more we need to stop engaging in things, occupations, hobbies that are no longer nourishing for our Light.

During these phases allow yourself to just melt, rest, sleep, provide all the support your body needs in every way. Let go of the need to do or be busy, let go of thinking that you aren't productive if you're not engaged in the old things, let go of holding on and controlling your body from what It's actually trying to do. Your LightBody is supporting you in so many ways if you allow it.

MEDITATE

Many of us started this journey the meditation route including myself. Many others didn't because they held resistance towards it or in some cases they felt like they had to meditate in a certain way. It wasn't until much later that I realized that meditation evolves into something more. There is a phase of the journey where you become so present and connected that each moment becomes a meditation, there is no separation anymore.

Many still get caught in the perception that in order to meditate one should listen to this, sit a particular way, breathe a certain way, clear your mind of all thoughts and if you can't do all of that then you can't or aren't meditating and therefore you fail at it. This is far from the truth. There is much more to meditation than just sitting still and chanting, and yet I'm not saying that it doesn't work because everything works; there is no right or wrong practice, better or less than either, they are all important.

The idea that I want to expand is that non-conventional styles of meditating are just as valid. Taking nature walks, swimming, being alone, writing, even playing can all things that one is called to do to reconnect.

Meditation is simply that, a practice in which we utilize to reconnect at a deeper level. If you take this and run with it there are thousands of things that you can choose to engage in that allow you to reconnect within. Anything that opens up your heart is a meditation, anything that brings you into a peaceful place inside is a meditation, anything that you enjoy and lifts you up is a meditation. Be open to this and get creative with it.

The Meditate State

These non-conventional meditative practices evolve in a way that you start to be in a meditative state more and more and more. When we think of meditation, we think of doing it for a certain amount of time and then you disconnect and go back to living your daily life. The point of it is actually to not disconnect but rather learn to stay in this space even after you stop doing the traditional form of meditation. This is about living, breathing, walking and interacting in a meditative state which is simply just being always open and connected.

This is we evolve out of the normal style of meditation and we transition fully into being in a meditative state all the time. When we meditate our brain waves reach a slower frequency of either alpha, theta and even delta at times. These slower frequencies allow us to be more relaxed, more connected and more open. Our conscious brain wave state is beta and most of us when we are in this state we function from fear because our conscious minds still operates from separation which is the same as fear and lack. It is a paradox because even though the beta brain waves are said to be the state in which we are awake and conscious it is actually when we are most unconscious because like previously mentioned we are still operating mostly from fear when we are awake. It's like we might seem like we are awake because our eyes are open and we can seem functional but yet the level of consciousness is very contracted and limited.

The brain waves that we reach while meditating is a much slower frequency where you are more relaxed, more creative, more imaginative, and this is where you get to reconnect with the deeper parts of yourself, the parts that you may not be fully conscious when you are operating from the beta brain waves. As we evolve and we start to activate our gamma LightBody we also start to function from a gamma brain wave. This brain wave has a much faster frequency than even beta but it also allows you to be in a much more receptive frequency and you are much more in-tuned with Higher States of Consciousness.

Open yourself up to new styles of meditation, open yourself up to being in a meditative and relaxed state more and more until it becomes part of your everyday existence. This is what we are all evolving into and becoming as Light Beings; always open, always connected, always in-tuned and always super conscious of everything.

SHINE

We are Stars, we are Suns, literally and as such we must shine, we've always done it no matter how bright or dim we have allowed ourselves to do it. Now throughout our existence we have dimmed our own Light because of the perceptions of others, because of the harsh realities that we chose and many more. We've always been Light we just grew scared of it and we suppressed it to the point that it has been detrimental to our bodies. Now more than ever we are starting to remember that we are Light and as such it is our Divine and innate purpose to Shine, not only a little but a lot, with our whole body and being.

We've been so locked up and suppressed that our Light has been very dim. Somewhere deep inside we unconsciously and subconsciously believed that shining our Light might be too much, too dangerous, too threatening and it may cause more attention that we can handle. We have grown accustomed to hiding, to being small, to being weak, to pretending and letting others shine. The ego is the aspect of ourselves that does all of these things because it perceives everything as a threat which it should hide from.

The reality is that nothing is truly a threat because you are everything; there is no separation at all. The things we fear are actually an aspect of ourselves that we are too scared to see, too scared to confront, too shy to become. The beauty is that now with all the Light pouring into this planet we are starting to see ourselves for who we truly are. We aren't small, we aren't powerless, we aren't weak, we aren't blind, but quite the opposite. When we live so immersed in the old 3D reality we lose ourselves, we forget who we are, who lose touch with our Soul, we function from a belief that follows old rules, regulations, mandates and lives in a box, a very tight box. This is literally hell. Yes, hell is right here on this plane, it isn't somewhere out there, it isn't somewhere you go after you transition if you break the rules. This was just a way to keep everyone from doing exactly that breaking the old rules, going against the norm, following their heart and Soul.

We are now feeling the dissonance that all of this has caused. We are starting to sense more how these systems have created much suppression and control and we are finally starting to break free. These old systems aren't based in purity, they are based on the separation that we have inside and all they do is create more and more separation, more judgment, more rules, more control and more manipulation.

The more amplified these distortions become the more our bodies are going to continuously feel how heavy all of these old systems actually are. When you connect more and more with your body, with your heart and Soul/Light you start to feel this, I don't have to tell you, you don't need to be convinced or forced into believing any of this because your own body and heart will tell you the more you open up and listen. Yes, the truth of everything is inside, you don't have to look for it "out there"; it is literally right below your nose. Your body is and has always been our truth detector, of course, none of us learned that, it's not something taught in schools, it is something that we come to remember when we open up fully and start breaking free from only believing in the old.

The journey of rediscovering yourself is the journey back to becoming your pure essence as Light; it is us remembering who we are and what we came here to do.

Our Purposes

We came here to be Light and to shine, it's simple, it's not complicated. Many of us get caught up in the belief that there must be more, that can't be my only purpose and in a way it is and it isn't. In fact, we have many purposes all throughout our life and yet they all deal with shining your Light. Because we've suppressed our Light so much, we've forgotten what it means to shine and be our pure Light that we must constantly remind ourselves, practice and become this Light in every way. As we continue to open up to our Light we start to receive the messages and the Divine guidance that will show us what else to do. Everything else becomes like icing on the cake because at a deep core level shining our Light is enough, being Light and sharing Light is enough. This is part of the BEing state, the phase where we recognize ourselves for exactly who we are and we remember that we are enough, we are perfect just as we are, just by being this Light; there is nothing less or nothing more we can do to be good enough or worthy enough.

The ways in which we can shine, be and share our Light are endless, they are infinite and we each came with certain innate skills, talents and gifts in which to shine our Light. The passions we chose to have are one of the many ways in which we start to shine our Light brighter; supporting others, assisting others, engaging in things that bring us much joy, peace and bliss are all ways in which we can shine our Light too. This is where the more we open up and become this pure Light fully, without the distortions, without the emotional attachments, without any of our ego constructs getting in the way as before, we start to receive the inner guidance that will tell us what else to do, where to shine our Light, what to focus our energy on, how to bring more Light into this world, how to support and assist others so they too remember and shine their Light as well. There are so many beautiful things that we all came here to do but the more you keep things simple and just focus on being and shining your Light the more we will remember all of our other purposes.

Don't get affixed to one thing though because it all changes. We don't come here with just one purpose or mission, we came here with many, we are meant to do many things and so the more you open up fully, become super present, detach from anything and everything you will be able to go with the flow as it all shifts, morphs and changes. Your Soul already chose specific things to do and accomplish prior to incarnating and so we have to fully honor and embrace that no matter how challenging it is for the ego. The ego might want to stay doing one thing, in one location, doing one purpose for the rest of its life but yet the Soul knows that it came here to be and do much more; so when you allow yourself to fully detach from everything even your passions and purposes you will be able to move a lot easier when you are guided to move and shift to a new purpose.

Keep yourself open at all times and allow yourself to embrace it all, enjoy it all and know that as you do the new purposes and new missions will bring even more magic, beauty and joy.

SHIFT

We are shape-shifters; we morph, transform, evolve and shift as we are guided because we are energy and as energy we are meant to always move. There is a negative connotation with this word that I feel it is appropriate to address. This word has brought much fear and much repulsion towards aspects of ourselves. Yes, everything that you perceive to be "out there", every character you perceive to be threatening, dangerous, evil is only but a reflection of all that you are. We are everything, we've been everything because as conscious energy we all come from the same source, we are all Source just experiencing itself in many different shapes, forms and levels of consciousness; there is no separation at all, only the one the fearful mind perceives.

Now, let's shift shall we…lol. As energy we are always moving, therefore we are always shifting. We have the ability to shift at will, shift energies, shift dimensionally, shift thoughts, shift perceptions, shift in any and every way… this is just who we are, period. Nothing can every change that. The more we absorb this and take it all in with the body not with the mind we are able to then remember that there is great power in this. Because we are this energy at our core, we then open ourselves to fully become it. If we need to shift emotions we do, if we need to shift aspects we do, if we need to shift perceptions, we shift; this is again part of us being shape-shifters. Yes, it is as simple as shifting from having a sad face to a happy face, shifting from walking to standing still, in fact it can even be a shift in energy that isn't even physically noticeable. We can shift from acting as our inner/wounded child into our Diving Child aspect. This becomes part of our pure power, it is part of our Mastery and one that we must learn to embrace.

Our old human/separated aspect doesn't know how to utilize this power in its favor and sometimes utilizes it unconsciously in a detrimental way. We have to move out of our old human ways and recognize that when we are operating from our old human mindset or aspect we can easily choose to shift into a Higher version of ourselves. It can be as simple as intending this and then choosing to do what is necessary to assist with this change. It can be as simple as remembering a funny memory, visualizing your favorite vacation spot, singing your favorite song, or anything that shifts your energy, relaxes your mind, opens your heart and brings you back into an allowing state where any of your Higher Self aspects can start to come through. Do you feel the fun and magic in that? This is what we are returning to so that we can always bring our Higher Self aspect to the table when we are engaging with others. This isn't to say that when a deep wound or emotion comes up that we should suppressed it because it isn't about that at all, it is more about being able to master our own energy in the ways that are most appropriate and respectful. If a deep emotion comes over me while I am engaging in a conversation or interacting with someone, I allow myself to not bring it forth, express it or violently release it in that moment because it wouldn't be appropriate, instead I allow myself to shift in that moment to a more calmer version of myself and when I am in a more appropriate space I can then release, feel, express what I need to in that moment so that my body can release it. This is about becoming fully responsible about dealing with our own heavy emotions that may come through, instead of just vomiting them on anyone that we come across because it would only create more chaos, imbalance and even cause harm. We are not here to disrespect or create more imbalances in ways that it can disrupt others; we are here to uplift, shine our Light and bring peace to world in every way that we are shown and guided. The more we take responsibility for our own energy and shift it as we are guided the more mastery we will have over ourselves.

TOOLS FOR ASCENSION

On this part of the book you will find only but a few tools that can assist you further in your own ascension journey. They will support, assist and activate you the more you open up to them and utilize them as you're guided in the way that you are guided to. Allow yourself to open up, play with them, utilize them in more than one way. Let these tools be but an activation of the many other ways that you can engage with them. Everything in some way will support you, sometimes there are things that you will be called to use more than others and so it's important not to become affixed or fixated to just one tool, or one way because there are countless tools and ways to utilize each tool.

Keep opening up and you'll start to see how everything supports you and the more you connect with all that supports the more your entire reality/Universe will keep showering you with infinite opportunities and possibilities that just keep loving and supporting you in every way.

Nature

Nature is one of the best activator that we start to utilize in our journey. Everyone has access to these frequencies and it is why it is something that I speak of and share so much, because there are virtually no excuses only the ones you create in your mind about not being able to spend more time in nature. Everyone has access to nature in some way because it is everywhere and that is the beauty of nature, its abundance is everywhere if you actually take the time to see it and connect with her.

Gaia as some of us call her is just pure frequencies of love, support, beauty, joy, simplicity and so much more. The more you open up to her the more your body will be able to retune, recalibrate, rebalance and repair at a deep cellular/DNA level. The tones, the sounds, the hues, the scents that Gaia brings are endless and so exquisite in every level; everything that she is offers a huge activation in every level when you allow yourself to receive it. In the old days we were so busy with our lives that we paid no attention to her, in fact we created realities that destroyed her and stripped her from so much and we all have to feel this fully so that we can come back to a place inside where we no longer allow this to occur. It takes every single person to start choosing differently, start becoming more conscious of how everything around them affects the environment and the planet. This is still our temporary home while in this body and so this is about coming into full consciousness of what's being done so that we start to correct it.

Nothing is too small or too insignificant it just takes us all to do our part and start making conscious choices to start assisting her more because the more we assist her and support her the more she supports us in every way that we need it.

Start opening up to these frequencies, start spending more time with her even if it's just outside in your own patio or backyard, you can even start bringing more of her into your home and space because the more that you do the more she will support your LightBody and your entire journey. You want to surround yourself with Gaia's tones and frequencies, colors and hues in every way because they will support you in recoding your body and field to where your entire reality gets upgraded and realigned in ways that support you. It may seem like a challenge or an expense but it is really an investment, you are investing more on you, your Light, your LightBody and this is what this whole journey is about, refocusing and repurposing your energy on you, honoring you, and allowing all that you need so that you can support others as well.

The whole planet is ascending and shifting in so many ways and so our continual reconnection with it will allow us to hold more of the New Earth grids inside our physical body. Gaia already holds the New

Earth/Crystalline grids and so now it is up to each and every single person on this planet to choose to hold these too by merging with her, becoming her and existing in a way that fully supports her.

Water

The frequency of water is extremely powerful in many ways. The soothing, calming, peaceful sounds and feelings that water activates within us is a necessity for each person. The more we utilize, activate and play with water the more we get to bring ourselves to a space inside that just flows; yes, we become like water, where we flow inside, we move and sway in a harmonious and synchronistic way that everything in our reality starts to reflect that. It doesn't matter how you are guided to play with water, what matters is that you open up these frequencies constantly and consciously so that you can allow them to activate more and more inside.

When I first started to connect more with water it was like I needed to be around it more, I would drive to the park more, walk to the lake, find waterfalls around where I lived and the peace that it would bring me was priceless, I didn't care how far or how long I needed to stay I just knew that I needed to be around water. Putting our body inside the water, swimming, soaking, bathing, wading, whatever you need to do to get you to really feel the activation is so very necessary. Allow your body to guide you through what it needs in every moment, let your head/linear mind rest and just go with the flow with everything even if it doesn't make a lot of sense, sometimes what doesn't make a lot of sense is exactly what you need in that moment.

So many of us took water for granted and we would take quick showers not realizing that taking that time as a sacred space to be with water, to reconnect with ourselves and merge with her is a very profound experience. Open yourself up to the abundance of water and how it is truly here to assist you; bring whatever you need in the shower or bath so that you can create this sacred experience for you in which you are fully submerged and engaged in and in a way that activates all of your senses. You'll start to have a much deeper connection with water and you'll also start treating her differently, with more honor, respect and appreciation to where you become more conscious of how you are utilizing her.

Rain is one of my favorites and snow is also but I am not in a place where it physically snows anymore so rain is the closest thing I have. When it rains I outside with her, playing, dancing, merging and connecting with her in every way I am guided, allowing my entire body to just feel these powerful purification frequencies that come from above is so magical. Let yourself be with nature in every way, let go of the fears or old beliefs, you are everything and the more you reconnect with it all the less you become fearful of it.

Fire

The element of fire is one that I started physically working with more in the latter phases of my journey and when I do I love it. We have a deep fire burning inside that is part of who we are as the sun, as Light and so I started to recognize how much this frequency is feared and rejected by many of us. From a very young age we realized what happens if we touch fire or get too close to it and so the physical reaction created much fear in our reality where it translated with fearing our own fire inside, our own power and our own brightness. Fire is powerful, it can destroy but it can also purify and so allowing ourselves to remember all the pure qualities of fire instead of holding on to the old beliefs and perceptions will assist us all in accepting and embracing more of what we are.

We are becoming this bright burning fire that is meant to shine bright and collapse all of the old systems. This is very literal in many ways as we hold the foundation of the old systems inside and so if you are starting to feel or sense the burning sensation inside in any part of your body just know that you are burning and purifying an enormous amount of density. It might seem weird and bizarre at first but keep embracing it and most of all keep tuning in and asking your body how to support it. There are many things that happen in our body and so this is just one of the many explanations, the best thing to do is keep listening and connecting with your body so that it can tell you what it needs you to do.

One of the many powerful ways in which to utilize physical fire is through burning ceremonies. One of the things I started doing just last year is every time I would need to write down all my feelings, emotions, thoughts that were coming from my lower self I would tear the paper after I was done and do a burning ceremony afterwards so that the fire can assist in burning and purifying deeper and deeper levels of my body. It was a practice I started doing daily or even multiple times a day that greatly assisted me in clearing and releasing deeper and deeper levels of all the emotional, mental and physical density that was still held inside.

Sun

The sun is also another extremely powerful one to connect with (are you getting the hint that EVERY single one is equally as powerful? lol). We are stars, literally, we are made up of the same elements as that of stars which is why we all come from the stars and the Universe; yes, we are everything. As we start to continuously open up to this we start to remember just how powerful, expansive and infinite we truly are, there is no separation at all. The sun being the closes start in our planet holds an enormous amount of power. Any activity that comes from the sun activates our Soul, some of us even started changing the spelling of solar to SOULar because of this reason.

The more we connect, merge and activate through the sun the more we start to shine in every way. This is another big fear factor to get over, the spending too much time outside, exposing ourselves to the sun too much, and so on, everything was part of the fear based programming that made us fear and reject the very same thing that would activate and wake us up.

Tune in to this and allow your LightBody to guide you in this process, the time of day and amount of sunlight that you need each day will vary and just allow yourself to listen, honor and follow that guidance. The more time you start spending with the sun the more you activate, the more you're able to hold more Light, the more your body awakens in every way and the more you'll become the sun, shining as bright as a star and not ever dimming it in any way.

Earth/Gaia

Any and every Gaian frequency is assisting us so much in every way. When we start to awaken and we realize that not only do we not fit in the 3D world but we're not supposed to fit either, we start to no longer try to fit in. We begin to detach from the hustle and bustle and being a part of the old world becomes less and less desirable; we no longer push or force ourselves to do things in order to be accepted or liked by others. We start to find peace in just being on our own and in our space.

Spending time in nature brings us into the space of pure peace. Connecting with her and all that she is nourishes our bodies and our Soul in ways that nothing else can. Reconnecting with her allows us to remember just how simple, pure and beautiful life can truly be. When we connect with nature it's like nothing else exists, the old 3D reality seems so far removed from this pure space and in many aspects it is. The closer we are to the purity of nature, the more connected we become with the purity of our Soul, our hearts and with our bodies. We also start to feel how heavy and discordant the 3D world is and we choose to be less and less apart of it.

The frequencies of Gaia activate New Earth inside, it brings us into a space of pure peace, harmony, magic and joy that already exists within. Our hearts open up in ways that assist us in becoming who we are and experiencing a completely different reality. One of the simplest ways to start experiencing New Earth is through the softness and beauty of Nature.

Connecting with the earth, the ground, the grass through our bare feet offers a powerful activation that allows us to feel loved and supported. Many people practice grounding and although that is a part of the process that can support us in feeling safe on this planet, we want to connect with the earth in a way that allows us to also expand our consciousness beyond the physical plane.

The more Light we hold the more our energy bodies expand and we will experience many sensations like gravity shifts, dizziness, a feeling of lightness as if we were floating and this is because we are. The more density we release at a cellular level the less anchored we are to the physical plane. Yes, we will still have a physical body after ascension but yet our energy is able to expand far beyond our physical form in ways that will feel like we are flying, floating and out of space. The challenge is being able to be in two places at once per se, being fully anchored in the body, feeling supported on this planet, feeling the love all around and at the same time being able to expand past your body, into the sky and fly like the earth angels that we are.

Sounds

Frequency plays a huge role in this entire journey. Since

everything is energy, everything has a frequency whether we hear it or not. There are many frequencies that are inaudible to the human ear at this moment and so we aren't aware of all the different frequencies around us that are in dissonance with our Light. This goes beyond music, sounds or tones, this goes much deeper; everything around us that is constructed from the fear and lack frequencies disrupt the internal flow of our bodies and shut down our DNA.

As we become more aware of these discordant frequencies we start to replace them with those that resonate more. There are a myriad of sounds that can assist us in returning our entire body to its pure harmonic state in every level. From nature sounds, solfeggio tones, harmonic melodies, binaural beats and so much more. At times we might only listen to these since even the old types of music that we used to hear seem very discordant and unpleasant to hear. We come to a point where we no longer listen to anything that disrupts our peace; anything from news, media, distorted music and lyrics, loud/noisy places, traffic, etc. This is where spending more time in nature assist us greatly as well. The sounds of animals, birds, the wind, water, and all things that are part of nature create a pure resonance, a harmonic melody that retunes our bodies and restores our Light.

Allow yourself to become more observant of the sounds around you not only with your ears but with every part of your body. Because we've been so shut off from our body we haven't been able to feel/sense/recognize the millions of discordant frequencies that are constantly being transmitted by our "outer" world. When we start to recognize and tune in deeper to the distortions of the "outer" world we then have a responsibility to tune deeper inside to see where they are originating from. Remember that everything you perceive to be "outside" of yourself is only a reflection of something you hold inside. So when you can match the frequency of that which you see/hear "out there" to a frequency inside of your body then you have the power to shift it from within you and then you'll start to see how your "outer" reality start to shift and morph as well into a completely different reality.

Open up your body more to sense more and allow your inner guidance to assist you in re-aligning everything in your reality so that everything becomes much more harmonious, peaceful, joyful and blissful in every way.

Visuals

There are many, many supportive visuals that you can work, play and start adding to your physical and multidimensional reality. Anything from adding more colors, sacred geometry, nature pictures, even just pictures or images of things that you love, that bring you joy, that open up your heart will greatly assist. It doesn't have to be spiritual per se, it can be as simple as adding objects and physical things into your reality that create a space of peace, love and joy. This is where your entire reality becomes an altar, it becomes part of your sacred space that you must upkeep and constantly tune in to see what needs to be shifted, removed or replaced.

Adding the frequencies of nature and elementals is a huge part of the process because of how much expansiveness and harmony they bring. If you have a lot of clutter, dust or disorganization in your personal environment then that visual does influence your body and therefore your reality. The more open, observant and connected you are to everything around you the more you'll start to feel what visuals are supporting you and which ones are affecting you. The constant cleaning, clearing and re-organizing of one's physical environment becomes a sacred practice instead of a mental disorder. This is part of being so super in-tuned with everything that if we constantly have to clean or shift the material things around us so that our bodies can support the realities that we are desiring to create then we won't judge ourselves for it; what others say, think or believe doesn't even bother us anymore because our bodies, our fields and our environment become a number one priority.

There are certain colors, tones and hues that we may be guided to work with when we are clearing or activating different vortexes or energy centers in our bodies. Working with specific colors will support in the activating of your Rainbow LightBody as well as each different

energy center or chakra that you may be working with. Open up to be guided to the physical and energetic colors, visuals, images that will best support you in that phase and you'll start to enjoy this process so much more.

LightBody Support

Our LightBodies go through so much and require a lot of support. There is an enormous amount of density held inside of our bodies that every muscle, organ, bone, cell and atom must go through some major clearing, purging, purification and recoding processes that go far beyond what we can currently comprehend. Listening and honoring our LightBody's needs is one of the most important things that we all are required to do. One because we have been doing the exact opposite with our bodies for so long that a reversal of these energies is necessary in every level.

Our bodies will need certain foods and supplements at different times and phases and so it is going to be super important that you continuously tune in and ask what it needs, how much, how long it needs it for and so forth. Again, this goes back to regaining trust in our bodies and in their Divine knowledge. Our minds may think they know what they need, others may think they know what our bodies need but it is always best to tune inside and be open to the guidance that our bodies transmit.

The continual clearing and detoxification of every organ is going to be something that we are all going to have to do at some level and in different phases. Remember that every system inside of the body is going to be reworked, rewired, recoded, reprogrammed, reconfigured, recalibrated, rebalanced in every level and in every way so the more you listen and honor what it needs the smoother and faster this process will be. Yes, sometimes it will be very physical, the sensations, clearings and expansions are extremely physical sometimes where you will feel discomfort and pain, this is normal. Your body isn't broken or sick, it is just going through an enormous amount of cellular clearing, expansion and so much more that you will feel it. The more you open up to this, honor, surrender and embrace the process the more you'll start to see the personal shifts and changes that will occur in every level of your reality.

There are so many things that go along with LightBody support that I will just mention a few. As your muscles begin to break down, break open, clear and expand adding a muscular system support is going to assist tremendously. Liquid or crystal magnesium is an important mineral to start adding in to your diet because it will help your muscles relax at a deep cellular level. I will add that most of the times the pill format of magnesium isn't as effective as the liquid or crystal form so try both. Another thing to mention is that magnesium will relax your entire muscular system in that you will start to flush a lot more and you may become more emotional too and this is all normal. Everything that was stored inside of your muscles that was heavy is finally releasing in every way possible so keep allowing it.

The other support that I invite you to look into is a nervous system support. Becomes of all the overwhelmingly suppressed emotions held inside of the body your nervous system might go into an overload. Adding a natural supplement will assist you in opening up this system more so that it doesn't create more imbalances. My favorite ones that you can look into are Schisandra and Ashwagandha but I am sure there are others you can try.

Ideally what you want to do is go through every body system and ask what each needs. Things like vitamin C, vitamin B complex, vitamin D, spirulina and so much more are going to greatly assist the LightBody upgrades. Don't affix to anything for things change, you may need a large dosage of one thing and then you may not need any at all, it truly all depends on what the LightBody needs in that moment, so continue to just open up to it more and more.

Oils

Oils are another supportive tool that can be used in many different ways. Lavender is one of my favorite ones to use to calm, relax and open up. Peppermint is another great one for any sort of ache or pain especially when we go through head expansion and third eye openings.

The properties of oils can assist greatly mainly in relaxing the body so that more Light can come through. Massage oils are also an amazing addition that you can start playing with so that your body receives that physical support that it needs through touch. There is so much that can be activated and released by you giving yourself a massage. Many of us think or feel like we have to go some place to get a massage but it is important to allow ourselves to do it too. We have to break free from the subconscious program that "touching ourselves" is wrong, dirty or sexually distorted. This is partly why many of us may not want to massage ourselves and so it is important to feel everything that comes with that so that we can break free from all of those old belief systems and physical support ourselves through our own personal loving touch.

Our bodies need so much love, care, gentleness, softness especially because none of us truly received this kind of pure love when growing up and so now it is up to each and every single one of us to do that for ourselves without waiting or expecting anyone else to do it for us. Open up to you and your body and start to reconnect with it more. Yes, every single one of us have body parts that we may not fully love, appreciate or respect and it is going to be truly important to feel everything that may be blocking us from fully loving and embracing every single part of our body. Don't compare your body with anyone else's and just open up to truly see your body for what it is, a sacred temple that you chose. Yes, you chose everything about your reality including the body. Start to open up to remember the purposes of each experience you had that relates to your body. Open up to all the things that your body is assisting and reminding you off so that you can continue to release all the heaviness and distortion and finally be able to see yourself through the Cosmic lens of purity, love and beauty.

Smudging

Smudging is another supportive tool along this journey. This activates our sense of smell which in turn can assist us in relaxing the body, opening up the neural pathways, opening up our third eye and our heart space and much more. Tune in to see which ones would best assist us; sage is a powerful one to utilize, palo santo has one of my favorite scents, incense sticks and so much more.

Bringing things into your reality that will activate and expand all your senses is crucial. The more sensory your experience is the more you open up your pathways and neural transmitters in ways that will recode your entire communication system.

Crystals

Crystals are another powerful tool. There are so many different types that are used for different purposes. Many people ask which ones they should use and which ones are best for certain things and my answer is always go with your own internal guidance. The crystal that you may need in that moment may be a different one than what someone else says or what the description of the crystal might also say. Again this is where learning to trust in ourselves and our bodies is imperative because your body will know exactly what it will need to open up and create the result that is highest aligned.

Andara crystals are a little different than your regular, earth-based crystals like quartz or amethyst. These are highly activating and advanced conscious beings that take the form of glass-like crystals. They are made up of many different elements and they each have a unique energetic frequency that can assist greatly in reconnecting with many different beings and energies that will support your ascension journey. There is definitely much more to them but one of the fascinating things about them is that because they are so advanced they can connect with higher realms of consciousness and therefore the energy that they transmit is always expanding and evolving in that you won't really outgrown them like you may do with other types of crystals. The technology of an andara crystal is far beyond this time and will greatly assist your LightBody in the clearing, cleansing and anchoring of higher dimensional frequencies in your body. The more you open yourself, work, play, activate, clear and connect with them the more they will assist in a vast variety of ways.

Most people are unaware of them as I was just a few years ago and so I invite you to feel into them and be open to working with them when you are being called. You can even start by just looking at pictures or videos of them and working with them in this way until you are ready to call them forth in their physical form.

Because they work with the LightBody they can actually become an extension of your LightBody and therefore assist you in anchoring New Earth foundations and gridding systems in a much more powerful way. Again the things you can do and the ways you can work with them are truly infinite and so powerful. Open up to them and you'll be shown and guided as to how they can assist you more throughout your journey.

WRITTEN SOUL/LIGHT ACTIVATIONS

I am Open

I open my mind to see,

I open my heart to feel,

I open all my senses and breathe in more Light.

I open up to the new.

I am open to the old and all the lessons it's brought me.

I open up to all versions of myself and see them for what they are without judgment.

I open up to the new versions of myself that are ready to come out and be seen.

I open up to all the deep suppressed emotions that I may still be holding on to. I won't judge myself but rather embrace every part of me, I won't judge the inner child that is only wanting to be loved, wanting to be seen and wanting to be heard.

I open up to allow my Divine Mother and Father aspect and forgive my human family for all that they could not give me.

I give myself permission to open my heart, body and mind to a new perspective, a new story, a new reality that is aligned with my Light and the truth of my Soul.

I give myself permission to move on and be free. I am no longer scared of freedom, nor scared of my Light. I am ready to embrace myself and my Light as the most loving and supportive force that exists.

I am ready.

I am ready.

I am ready.

Repeat this activation, feel in your core, say it aloud and if/when guided record it and listen to it when you're guided and let the frequencies anchor and activate deeper into your cells.

You Are Fully Supported

Open your heart and mind to see.

Open your heart and body to feel.

Open your higher heart and mind to remember.

Shift your focus to this now.

Shift your energy to this moment.

Feel your body and everything around you.

Connect with the things, objects, frequencies that surround you.

Feel how them in their highest vibration and feel how they are supporting you.

They are supporting you in seeing more, feeling more, sensing more, sharing more, remembering more, releasing more and realigning everything back to purity.

You chose everything in your reality to support you.

Allow your inner child to open its heart and start remembering, remember those times when you were in your joy, when you were in play, when you were in your fun, hold on to that frequency of support and bring it into this now moment.

Start to activate this frequency deeper and deeper within and be open to feeling and releasing everything that is not aligned with this frequency as well.

Start to feel what truly supports your Light and what doesn't, what keeps you suppressed, what keeps you in fear, what keeps you locked up inside and hiding... what keeps you thinking and believing that you aren't fully supported.

What version of yourself doesn't believe that You can or should be supported, what version of yourself doesn't think it deserves to be supported, what version of yourself doesn't want to be supported, doesn't want to change or open its heart.

Feel into everything because every version of yourself exists inside of you, whether you're conscious of it or not.

Feel into the thoughts, feelings, emotions... feel your body, feel your bones and allow these lightcodes and frequencies to go deeper inside.

Breathe in and open up.

I am ready to feel everything to my core.

I am ready to allow everything to be shown to me so that I can remember more.

I am ready to follow, honor my Higher Self fully.

I am ready to listen to my Light instead of my ego.

I am ready to fully surrender and be fully supported because as Light it's what I am.

I am the frequency of support, I am the frequency of pure love and compassion, I am the frequency of benevolence and embrace.

I am fully ready to be all that I am.

I am ready.

I am ready

I am ready.

Breathe it all into your core and fully allow the recoding of your field.

Read this aloud and as often as you're guided.

Continual Rebirthing

I open myself in this now

I open myself to all that's pure

I open myself to my Light

I open myself to my breath

Every day is a new day, a new flow and new vibration and the more I open up to it the more I see/the magic in it.

The old me is fading away, it is becoming just a glimpse and a memory, it is no longer holding the power it once had on me. It is fading, vanishing and dissolving from my very cells, muscles and DNA. It was just a version of myself that I respect and that I am fully ready to transcend.

I am opening up more each day to this new me, the true me, the original me that holds all as sacred.

I am opening up each day to a new flow, new ideas, new ways of being and new ways of sharing. Yes it's a bit challenging at times but I'm not alone and I am in no rush, I just open up myself a little more and a little more each time and feel all that comes.

There is nothing to hide anymore, nothing to suppress, nothing to dim and nothing to oppress for there is no shame or guilt in all that I chose because that was part of my path and part of my Soul.

I am now reviving myself, rebirthing in each way, every day and in every moment and although it feels like I'm meeting this version for the very first time it's an essence that's always been with me, it's always been inside and the more I connect with it the more I remember and the more I embrace it in every way.

There is a feeling deep inside that knows, that truly remembers and is fully ready and I must connect with it in every way.

I am ready to the continual rebirth of all that I am.

I am ready.

I am ready.

I am ready.

Breathe it all into your core and fully allow the recoding of your field.

Read this aloud and as often as you're guided.

The BridgeKeeper of Worlds

I am the Bridgekeeper of my own reality.

I am the WayShower to a new reality.

I am becoming more and more conscious of who I am and my role in this reality.

As I open up my heart to all that I am I become fully emerged in this present moment and each cell and molecule in my body is activated to its divine truth and purity.

As I open up my whole body/heart and field I become one with all that is.

I am not separate and I never truly was.

It was only part of the game that we all consciously chose to play.

Nothing was ever truly done to me but for me.

It was the unconscious mind that was so strong that it made me believe in the harshness of this world.

I am now ready to break free from the chains and bonds of this illusion.

I am ready to be who I truly am in every way.

I open my heart and mind so that it all re-aligns back with my light.

I open up my field to received more of these pure, Light encoded frequencies that are here to support me and break the old DNA chain and activate my 12 strand and beyond.

I am ready to see everything that is still keeping me in fear, in lack and in the old illusion of truth.

I am no longer allowing myself to support the old ways and I give myself permission to dissolve all the separation inside more and more and more.

I am ready to breathe more Light.

I am ready to anchor more Light.

I am ready to become Light.

Breathe it all into your core and fully allow the recoding of your field.

The Master In You

The Master in you is awakening, remembering, coming alive and coming into its power.

We've always been but we forgot.

We were told you weren't good enough, not smart, not beautiful and not worthy. But we always knew that wasn't true. We knew deep down there was more to us, there was something out of sync with what we were being taught. It's become more and more apparent how polar opposite all of that was and we are returning to our pure mastery.

We are learning how to stand in our own power, learning how to speak through love, learning how to stand up for ourselves through our pure strength, we are learning to hold honor and respect for all that was and all that is still for it served many purposes.

We are NOW ready... ready to be more, open more, create more and do more.

We are ready to transform into the beautiful and powerful Masters that we are, we are no longer needing to play small, fit into the societal boxes, sing their song, play their games, or follow their rules because we came here to create all new...

We are the ones that will set us free... the ones that are cosmically aligned with our purity and our love... the ones that support us in every way and much more.

We are waking up.

We are remembering how to live as Love, how to exist as peace, how to embrace as Light, how to share as abundance, how to support while empowering others as well.

We came here to be Masters and activate the ones that are ready.

We are ready.

Breathe it all into your core and fully allow the recoding of your field.

Read this aloud and as often as you're guided.

We Are Energy

We are energy.

We are this sacred space of infinite energy.

As we unlock more of this truth from deep within us our Light becomes bigger, brighter and stronger. As our Light awakens, it beings to spin faster, move faster and our frequency begins to increase. In this beautiful space we have access to more information. When we stand still and pause we open our hearts and expand our vision. We become more aware of our surroundings, we become more aware of our decisions, we become more aware of our intentions, we become more aware of our actions, we become more aware of why we do the things we do and we start to feel the alignment or misalignment.
We become more respectful of our Light and our energy and we begin to break free from anything and everyone that does not serve our purpose, amplify our Light and support our purity.

In this NOW moment of stillness everything dissolves, I am no longer choosing to compromise my own Diving Light with unconsciousness. I no longer choose to hold space for separation. I choose to see the separation within myself, see the aspect that is still holding that belief and allow it to come back home. I bring myself back to this pure state of being, knowing and existing that is held within my own Higher Heart. I now bring everything back into my own pure heart. I dissolve all walls, chains, blocks of separation and choose to be still with it all.

I now remember that my pure essence, my Divine Heart is always open if I allow it. And once I allow my heart to open, everything that is not Light starts to dissolve. This is the beginning of a continuous space of just being. There is no lack, no fear, no judgment in this space. There is no fault, forgiveness or falseness in this space because all experiences are valid and served a purpose. There is only energy, only Light, only peace in the remembrance of who I really am.

As I begin to sit still, be still, walk in pure presence, do in full awareness my energy and my Light being to radiate brighter and stronger than ever before. This being state merges into my every word, action and thought and I being to embody it fully. The Being state is not just about doing nothing even though it does start that way for many people. We have to first break the cycle and pattern of always doing something by just being still and not doing anything at all but sitting with nature, staring at the sky, breathing fresh air and then in that state you begin to access new ideas, new inspirations, new remembrance of what to do, what to release, what to focus on. Our Divine Masculine begins to activate, it beings to merge with the body, the soul and our energy. This holds the frequency of sacred action and it becomes one with the Divine Feminine, sacred presence and Divine Child, pure inspiration.

I allow this stillness to unlock new possibilities, new adventures, new dreams, new visions and new action steps for me to follow. As I begin to remember and activate more and more on deeper and deeper levels I begin to hold the present of this now in every moment and in everything that I do. Every aspect of me becomes whole, every aspect of me becomes unified, every aspects of me begins to grow, expand and evolve.

The more I sit still, the more I choose to do only the things that amplify my Light. At first these things are simple and may seem small but they hold much greatness in my journey. I won't start by doing a lot, in fact quite the opposite, the things that bring me peace and harmony, are simple, they are free and they are available in all moments. This is part of the new way of existing as pure conscious humans. We completely dismantle our old structures and our old patterns and we begin to allow a new sense of belonging, a new expanded way of perceiving.

We are all evolving. Everything is evolving and as we allow this natural flow we being to access more and more and more of our sacred knowing.
Allow yourself to be, allow yourself to align your energy and your actions with your divine power and everything will change within and without.
Remember that everything is held deep within you and you are ready to access it all.

Breathe these codes and sequences deeper within and open up for the continual recalibration of your entire human template.

Give Yourself Permission

I am fully ready to give myself permission...permission to be more, see more, feel more, become more, release more and embody more of my purity.

I am fully ready to give myself permission to no longer support, feed, engage, amplify the old structures and systems. I am ready to release myself fully from them and open up to the new systems, the new open and expansive ways of living and existing.

I am fully ready to give myself permission to feel all that I still hold inside, see all the separation that I still have within and open myself more and more to no longer carry it inside of my body.

I am ready to be me, to be Light, to be pure Love, to be peace and the be joy that I truly am.

I am ready to dissolve the old perceived past and illusion that kept me bound to a version of myself that was only temporary. I am ready to stand as my Light, share my Light and support myself as pure Love.

I am ready to open up fully to all that I am, all that I came here to be and do and all that I came here to share and support.

I am ready to be Light in every way and in every existence.

I am ready, I am ready, I am ready.

Breathe these codes deeper and deeper within and allow your body to continuously release all that it needs to.

Keep Going!

Light codes are truly infinite; there are so many, so vast, so complex and so powerful in many ways. These are just but a few that can assist and support you in opening you more to this journey. The light encoded frequencies that are pouring through the planet at this time are truly changing everything in the most powerful and profound ways, we just have to keep opening up to them.

This journey isn't easy all the time in fact it will test you and challenge you in ways that you've never been testing before. Every limiting belief, liming mentality, limiting program that you have inside of your body will be triggered, activated and challenged in every way so that you no longer operate from the old systems. We are not here to follow or support the old anymore, we are here to live New Earth fully in every way.

Open yourself up to the new ways, the new foundations, the new programs, the new systems that are being recoded inside your physical body because this is what is truly going to make the difference. Our physical world isn't going to become New Earth until we do, we must first become New Earth, become the Light, become the pure Love and the peace that we desire to experience on this planet. It is truly an individual choice that ripples out in to the grids and transforms everything... and it all starts with you.

Keep opening up, keep allowing more, keep embracing more, keep feeling more, keep clearing more, keep honoring it all and you'll start to see and feel how everything begins to change in every way, in every level and in every aspect of your reality.

Are you ready to go all in?

If so, I'll see you on the other side... the New Earth/Heaven side!

Support Opportunities

Light Encoded Articles

Quantum Light Activations

Personal Energy Sessions

Group Support Sessions

Books

YouTube Videos and Lives

Courses

And more available at

www.AwakenDeeperWithin.com

For Spanish Support visit:

www.DespiertaTuSol.com

ABOUT THE AUTHOR

Samantha SolBright Rodríguez is a New Earth Guardian, Wisdom Keeper, LightKeeper, Ascension Guide, Author, WayShower, Ascended Being and Activator of Higher Consciousness.

Born in Mexico she left at the age of nine to the US with her family. From an early age she didn't align with the traditional way of living of going to school, getting a high paying job and having a family. There was something more to what she wanted to BE and do. In spite of that she ended up going the normal school path and went off to college.

After college she spent five years discovering new passions and learning about dance, home business, marketing and live events but yet she never found true fulfillment. It wasn't until the summer of 2015 when she started to meditate and dive deeper into the world of spirituality and energy that she started to remember what she had forgotten.

Shortly afterwards she had a spontaneous "Galactic Awakening and Expansion," which flipped her world upside down, throwing her even deeper to an even more fascinating world that deep down she knew was true. She continued on a journey of self discovery, diving into her intuitive gifts and abilities, connecting with spiritual guides and finally deciding to go "all in" on her physical ascension journey, leaving everything behind in 2020.

As she continues to evolve, expand, remember and fully ascend in her physical body she assists, supports, guides and activates others in re-discovering and remembering who they are and the power of the essence they hold. She currently resides in Mexico where she brings forth Higher Wisdom, codes, keys and tools through her videos, courses, and writings to assist humanity in the personal and global shift in consciousness.

For more guidance and support visit her website at
http://AwakenDeeperWithin.com.

For Spanish support visit:
http://DespiertaTuSol.com

BOOKS BY THIS AUTHOR

LIVING AS PURE LOVE

DESCRIPTION: We are waking up and remembering that there is more to who we are and what we are capable of. As we open our hearts and minds we start to feel the pure essence that we are. We aren't just this human body; we aren't small, weak, alone or separated but quite the opposite. As we dive deeper into our own self re-discovery journey we start to dissolve the old constructs, beliefs and identities of who we thought we were. It's time to remember and live as who we were always meant to BE, as the pure, infinite, expansive, powerful and abundant essence of Love.

VIVIENDO COMO AMOR PURO

DESCRIPCION: Estamos despertando y recordando que somos y tenemos la capacidad de mucho más. Entre más abrimos nuestro corazón y mente sentiremos al esencia pura que somos. No nada más somos un humano en un cuerpo; no somos pequeños, ni débiles, ni separados ni estamos solos pero todo lo contrario. Entre más nos sumergimos en nuestro camino y nos volvemos a descubrir comenzaremos a disolver todos los constructos, creencias e identidades viejas que creíamos ser. Es tiempo de recordar y vivir como la esencia pura, infinita, expansiva, poderosa y abundante que siempre hemos sido destinados a ser.

Made in the USA
Middletown, DE
05 September 2022